SIX PRINCIPLES
OF THE
DOCTRINE OF CHRIST

Foundation of the Pentecostal Apostolic Faith

2nd Edition

HARRY L. HERMAN, D.D., TH.D.

EDITOR-IN-CHIEF
Eric A. Beda, MBA

ALPHA OMEGA
PUBLISHING

Copyright © 2017 by Alpha Omega Publishing Company

All rights reserved.

No part of this document may be reproduced or transmitted in any form or by any means, electronic, mechanical, photocopying, or recording without prior written permission from Alpha Omega Publishing, except in the case of brief quotations embedded in critical articles and reviews.

Published in the United States by
Alpha Omega Publishing Company
P.O. Box 353, Jackson, MI 49204

Library of Congress Control Number: 2017939288

ISBN: 978-0-9985799-3-1

All Scripture quotations are derived from the Holy Bible, King James Version.

Alpha Omega Publishing Company publishes books that promote the discussion and understanding of the Pentecostal movement throughout the world since the Day of Pentecost. These books are made possible by the enthusiasm of our readers; the support of a committed group of donors, large and small; the collaboration of our many partners in the independent media and ecclesiastical organizations; booksellers, who often hand-sell Alpha Omega Publishing books; librarians; and above all by our authors.

Books may be purchased in quantity and/or special sales by contacting the publisher:

Alpha Omega Publishing
E: info@omegapublishing.org
www.omegapublishing.org

Printed in the United States of America

These principles lay the foundation of the New Testament church teachings.
-- Bishop Ira Combs, Jr.,
Greater Bible Way Temple, Michigan

A powerful book that will move the teacher and the student to action in their walk with God.
-- Pastor Tony Thomas,
Christ Temple, Michigan

Wow! I just finished reading this book! I feel like I've learned more in this book than I did in almost 35 years since my own spiritual birth! Biggest lesson - repentance is NOT a one-time event - it's something we must do consistently.
-- Charles, Michigan

I am so glad I read this book. I am learning so much information. This is a very powerful subject.
-- Lisa, Tennessee

I have truly enjoyed this book.
-- Dr. Anthony Buckles, MD,
Family Practice/ Emergency Room Medicine, Illinois

I have enjoyed my study of the Principles of the Apostolic message and have gained more insight in my faith and a new resolve for the truth.
-- Mrs. LaMarr, Maryland

The teachings and revelations found in this book are astonishing.
--Bishop Tim Obidike, Nigeria

I appreciate the simplistic layout of the information. There is a huge wealth of information in the book.
-- Amy, Michigan

This book has enabled me to learn about God's order and plan. These principles have been key to unlocking the revelation of what is in God's Holy Bible.
-- Pastor Radar Johnson,
Greater Bethel Temple, Kentucky

This book is dedicated to the men and women who are new to the Christian faith and for young ministers to use as a tool to better understand the Pentecostal Apostolic message.

ACKNOWLEDGMENTS

First of all, this work is dedicated to my Lord and Savior, Jesus Christ, whose Spirit of inspiration and revelation is the source of the contents of these writings.

Furthermore, I would like to dedicate this book to my wife, Dr. "Jerry" Herman for her generous expertise in editing the first edition of my writings. She was never too busy to help me in any way possible. It was her encouragement that prompted me to put the basics of the teaching so dear to both of us on paper.

This book is also dedicated to those learned and scholarly Bible teachers, who taught me so fervently in my formative years. Their lessons have not and will not be forgotten for they have instilled in me a knowledge and understanding of God through the inspired instruction of the Holy Ghost. Most have gone to be with the Lord, but the legacy of their ministry lives on to instruct and inspire a new generation of believers. It is my hope that this book, *"Six Principles of the Doctrine of Christ"* will be a channel through which the teachings of the "Fathers" may pass on to generations to come.

PREFACE

Whom shall he teach knowledge? And whom he make to understand doctrine? Them that are weaned from the milk, and drawn from the breasts.

Isaiah 28:9

When you think of the *Six Principles of the Doctrine of Christ*, think of foundation, building blocks, knowledge, understanding, wisdom. Think of revelatory truth. The success of this book since its first publication underscored a genuine appetite for deep and revelatory knowledge about the right division of the Word concerning the gospel of Jesus Christ. With numerous voices around the belief in baptism and infilling of the Holy Spirit, it is needful to have scriptural understanding of these subjects.

This book is written for individuals who crave the pure spiritual milk of the Word, so that by it, you may grow up in salvation and serve God wholeheartedly according to the right division of the Scriptures (1 Peter 2:2). This work is very precious to new ministers and new converts who will find this book as a valuable resource in understanding the basics of the Pentecostal Oneness (Apostolic) message. The wise writer Solomon wrote, *"wisdom is the principle thing; therefore get wisdom: and with all of thy getting, get an understanding"* (Proverbs 4:7). A house without a stable foundation is destined to fall and be destroyed. These principles provide a foundation to begin building a new life in Christ and help develop an effective ministry which is pleasing and acceptable to God.

The principles provide believers with a platform and a blueprint for the ministry of Christ. If these principles are in you and abound, you will be neither barren nor unfruitful in the knowledge of our Lord Jesus Christ (2 Peter 1:8). It is my hope and prayer that this book equips and empowers you to develop a lifestyle that is inculcated in the work of the Apostolic Fathers.

Elder Eric Beda,
Editor-in-Chief

SIX PRINCIPLES
OF THE
DOCTRINE OF CHRIST

CONTENTS

Acknowledgments — V

Preface — Vi

Introduction — 1

1 Repentance from Dead Works — 5

2 Faith Toward God — 19

3 Doctrine of Baptisms — 25

4 How Were You Baptized? — 33

5 Laying On Of Hands — 41

6 The Holy Ghost: God's Promise — 49

7 Resurrection Of The Dead — 61

8 Eternal Judgment — 75

9 Striving For Perfection — 85

Author — 97

Afterword — 99

Notes — 101

INTRODUCTION

This book will deal with the principles of the doctrine of Christ as outlined in Hebrews 6:1-2,

> *Therefore leaving the principles of the doctrine of Christ, let us go on unto perfection; not laying again the foundation of repentance from dead works, and of faith toward God of the doctrine of baptisms, and of laying-on of hands, and of, resurrection of the dead, and of eternal judgment.*

The substance of this book is especially important for newly converted Christians to become acquainted with the Apostolic message. It is referred to by theologians as the Pentecostal Oneness faith, the Apostolic faith, or simply the Apostolic Doctrine. The fundamentals of the Apostolic teachings are treated with considerable detail. Going or striving toward perfection and holiness is part of this study.

Let us first define the word "principle". Principle comes from a Latin word, "principium", which means beginning; it includes the comprehensive and fundamental law, doctrine, or assumptions. Doctrine simply refers to something that is taught. The principles of the doctrine are the beginning, fundamental, and foundation teachings taught by the Apostolic fathers and shared through Apostolic succession. The principles are the starting point of a path that leads to perfection. All Oneness teachings are founded on these principles.

The six principles are listed in Hebrews 6:1-2.

1. Repentance from dead works.
2. Faith toward God.
3. Doctrine of baptisms.
4. Laying-on of hands.
5. Resurrection of the dead.
6. Eternal judgment.

These six principles are the basics of what we believe and are important for any growth toward staying saved. There is however, a seventh principle, "going onto perfection". It goes beyond the first six, for without the first six, there is no foundation for the seventh. As you review these principles, the goal of perfection or maturity is in view. The objective is to become full-grown, mature children of God with the ability to reflect the character of His righteousness and holiness in this world, and preparing for the world to come. These principles are progressively linked to together. If we look at the six principles as an ascending staircase, it becomes apparent that before the second principle can be acted on, the first must be obtained. For example, before one can have faith toward God, there must be a turning away from the dead works of our present life coupled with a change of attitude toward God.

Water baptism would be an exercise of futility if there did not exist a belief in God and an expectation of receiving something from Him (Hebrews 11:6). Water baptism is a cleansing process which requires faith in the shed blood of Jesus who died that whosoever believes might receive forgiveness and remission of sins. This step points toward a power received from God, which is the Holy Spirit, enables one to live free from sin. The Holy Spirit or the Holy Ghost is the assurance of eternal life after death. If our hope was centered only in this life, then we are most miserable indeed (1 Corinthians 15:19). Therefore, the doctrine of the resurrection is the next step to take. Our proof and hope are centered in Jesus Christ, who we must believe rose from the grave and is alive forever more. Without these principles, nothing in the future is relevant. Before we grow into mature children of God, the principle of eternal judgment must be firmly in place as the final step of the staircase. Eternal judgment establishes the actions of God against sin and provides a motivation to love and serve God. Living to please God will have its reward because, at the final judgment, a separation will be made between good and evil, and the righteous and the wicked. The righteous and good will be rewarded with life whereas the wicked and evil with eternal damnation.

Eternal judgment exemplifies the righteousness of God, who will not destroy the righteous with the wicked because all will have their appropriate reward, which is life or death (Genesis 18:23-25). These principles are the basis of the Apostolic faith and cannot be expounded until they become the fundamental beliefs of the heart. Other aspects of the faith or goal of spiritual perfection hinge on believing these principles. Notice the apostle's statement, leaving the principles of the doctrine of Christ, let us go onto perfection or full-growth. He is not saying let us forget this foundation, but the greater doctrine of belief is in the doctrine of Christ. To know Christ according to Scripture, one must first believe these fundamental principles. He is involved with each, but there is more to knowing Christ than repentance, faith toward God, baptism, and etc. The apostle said, believe these first, stand firm on them, do not be "carried away with every wind of doctrine, by the sleight of men, and cunning craftiness" (Ephesians 4:14) but don't stay just on the foundation of the house, go on and build the house because there are greater knowledge of Christ.

Apostle Paul lets us know that the main objective is to know Christ and "the power of His resurrection" (Philippians 3:10). The goal of the ministry is to bring the people of God into the full knowledge of His will, and to know the hope of His calling, and the glory of His inheritance in the saints (Ephesians 1:18), and to acquire the knowledge of the Son of God (Ephesians

4:11-16). Before this can happen, these fundamentals must be believed.

Jesus Christ is the focal point of each of these six principles. When the gospel is preached and obeyed, repentance is the result as one turns from sin toward Christ. Jesus is the name and His shed blood is the means by which sins are remitted. The whole process is started because of our faith toward the Son of God, Jesus Christ. Jesus is the giver of the Holy Ghost, which is the Spirit of Christ sent down from Heaven as on the Day of Pentecost. It is the same spirit received by believers when the apostles laid hands on them and it is the same spirit received by believers today. The resurrection of Jesus Christ provides the reason for one to believe in the resurrection as a fact.

Jesus will be sitting on His throne to judge all the souls of mankind ever born at the final judgment (Acts 17:31; John 5:22-30). If we believe these principles, then we must believe in Jesus as the Scriptures declare Him to be (John 7:38).

Since these principles are the basic teachings of Christ, who is the foundation or the rock the church is built on, then it is absolutely essential that this foundation is firmed and unchanged if it is to be victorious over the assaults of the gates of Hell (Matthew 7:24-27; Matthew 16:18). These principles need no updating, revisions or additions, but must remain as they were first taught by Jesus Christ and the apostles, the doctrine on which Pentecostal Apostolics stand (Ephesians 2:20-22). This is the faith once delivered to the saints (Jude v. 3). New generation of preachers may change them to suit their needs, but to do so would give the enemy, Satan, a sure victory. Having set forth these six principles of the Pentecostal Apostolic message, let us now proceed to examine each in detail.

PRINCIPLE I

~1~
REPENTANCE FROM DEAD WORKS

Repent and turn to God, and do works befitting repentance.

-- Acts 26:20

Repentance is more than just simply turning away or ceasing from wrongdoing. It is a change of heart and attitude toward misconduct and not simply fearing the consequences of it. One must come to recognize that they are wrong and their path is unproductive, and lifeless before the Almighty God. It is mandatory to completely turn around before any contact can be made with God.

Repentance has always been a fundamental part of building a relationship with God. It is a fundamental principle in the Old and New Testaments. It is the one thing God expects of anyone who intends to walk with Him. Before repentance can become a fact, the gospel must first be preached and believed. One repents because they are ready to turn from sin and serve God. The psalmist said, "*I am ready to halt, and my sorrow is continually before me. For I will declare mine iniquity; I will be sorry for my sin*" (Psalm 38:17-18).

The ministry of John the Baptist began with "*Repent, the Kingdom of God is at hand*" (Matthew 3:2), Jesus began His ministry with "Repent and believe the gospel" (Mark 1:15), and Jesus ends His ministry with "*Repentance and remission of sin should be preached in his name among all nations beginning at Jerusalem*" (Luke 24:47).

Repentance means to change one's mind and purpose. It carries the sense of regret and remorse for the lifestyle one has lived. Repentance is a change of heart and attitude toward the things practiced that are offensive to God. Particularly, it is a change of heart from the practice of what one comes to know as sin. True repentance reproduces fruit as an evidence of the change made. Practically, the lifestyle once loved is now hated and the practices of the past are forsaken. There is a recognition of the depraved sinful condition before God and one is willing to make a complete break with the past to serve Him. The attitude of the penitent sinner is, Lord, I am all wrong and you are all right, and I am willing to forsake my way to walk in your path. Many coming from other faiths to accept the Apostolic message still carry residual opinions from their past religious experience and do not always totally forsake them. Until there is complete submission to God's way these opinions will hinder growth, resulting in spiritual weakness and the loss of many benefits God promised. No one can prosper with a divided mind.

The prophet lays the basis for repentance, "*Let the wicked forsake his way, and the unrighteous man his thoughts: and let him return unto the Lord, and he will have mercy upon him; and to our God, for he will abundantly pardon*" (Isaiah 55:7). Forsaking is the key to repentance. To be sorry is one thing, but to forsake produces a change of heart and attitude. One must forsake the past because their values of good do not measure up to God's values. If repentance is to be a fact, then one must come into the knowledge of a better way. Despite the good report from God (Job 1:1; 1:8), Job had a flaw and when confronted by God he admitted it, "*Behold, I am vile, what shall I answer thee? I will lay my hand on my mouth. Once I have spoken, but I will not answer: yea, twice, but I will proceed no further*" (Job 40:4-

5). He then concludes "*Wherefore I abhor myself, and repent in dust and ashes*" (Job 42:6).

Repentance is from 'dead works', but just what are dead works? Dead works are first and foremost sin. *"All have sinned and come short of the glory of God"* (Romans 3:23). Second, they are the works of the flesh or the conduct that separates man from God as a result of our corrupt and fallen nature. Third, they are religious ordinances that do not produce life (*i.e.* observing the Jewish Law or meaningless rituals so deeply embedded in religious practices, or cultures). They are religious beliefs and practices, opinions, and cherished goals that take individuals away from God.

Dead works are works without life and can produce no life (godliness, righteousness, and holiness). It is impossible for things without life to bear fruit. Dead fruit trees remain dead, both summer and winter. In the garden, Adam first sinned by choosing to disobey God's command not to eat of the fruit of the tree of the knowledge of good and evil (Genesis 2-3). Only one law to be obeyed, but Adam failed and as a result became separated from God. The sin of disobedience became deeply embedded in his nature, a nature passed on to all his posterity. Only God can produce life and separation from Him generates death. Adam's sin passed the death sentence onto mankind. Man is unprofitable to God in his natural state. In the process of Adam's sin, two conflicting wills came into existence: the will of God and the will of man. As long as these two wills conflict there can be no peace between man and God. Since God is sovereign, then we must surrender to His will. The first step toward any reconciliation with God is repentance. Man must yield to God by turning from his will and submit to God's will.

Both sin and the works of the flesh must be rejected if repentance is to be a fact. But just rejecting sin is not enough, one must turn to God who can produce life in these dead members (Ephesians 2:1-2). Life is not generated by man, but from God to man. The word "repent" or its derivative first appeared in the Book of Genesis (6:6), where the term is used to express God's grief at the depraved, wicked, and evil condition of man. God changed His mind toward man and abandoned His intention to destroy man. The life savior of the human family was Noah, who found grace in the sight of God. He was different from the rest of his generation, his faith and lifestyle pleased God. If man is not grieved over his wrong doing, then any change will be meaningless and insincere.

Sin is the fulfillment of our will and no matter how good our works of righteousness may be, it is impossible to generate life from dead resources. "*In me, (that is, in my flesh) dwelleth no good thing*" (Romans 7:18). In fact, the Prophet Isaiah declared that man's righteousness is as filthy rags, repugnant, and contemptible (Isaiah 62:6).

Apostle Paul describes the works of the flesh as "*the motions of sin, which were by the law, did work in our members to bring forth fruit unto death*" (Romans 7:5). The law revealed God's purpose for man and provided knowledge of what was sin (Romans 3:20). However, the law made no provision for the deliverance of man from the bondage of sin. It only held captive those who were under its dominion, but with the advent of Christ and His shed blood, an atonement for our condition was provided at last. All mankind can turn to Jesus Christ for deliverance and escape the slavery caused by sin (Romans 7:6). For this deliverance to become a reality, one must choose to leave sin and accept deliverance. The Mosaic Law was a system of self-help and will power which produced nothing more than dead works. There was no change in the nature of the people of that era, having to repeat the Atonement Sacrifice year after year. Paul, the staunch religious man that he was, came to realize his religious background as a Pharisee was counter productive to good works and was willing to "count it all loss for Christ" (Philippians 3:3-9). After his encounter with Jesus on the road to Damascus, Paul realized his need to change. It was evident to him that he did not please God, contrary to his good intentions.

Sin, as we commonly think of sin, was not the ultimate issue. The issue was Paul's righteousness based on observing the secret writings of the Old Testament rather than God's righteousness through Jesus Christ. It was his will against God's will. It was his practice against God's practice and finally, the boasting of his life against the life of Christ. When Paul realized that his life under the law was insufficient, he readily repented and placed his faith in the works and power of Jesus Christ (Acts 9:1-20). He emphatically declared that "we have no confidence in the flesh" because putting trust in the flesh would only produce dead works (Philippians 3:3-9). This is true today among those who profess christianity. People hide behind religious fidelity to a doctrine of their choice. They boast of values of morality, honesty, integrity and good works, not knowing that without the sacrificial life of Christ and being filled with the Holy Spirit all their good works will not bring them eternal life. Good works do not come from self but are the product of Christ in us (Ephesians 2:10).

The works of the flesh, the product of human nature are listed in the Book of Galatians (5:19-21): adultery, fornication, uncleanness, lasciviousness, emulation, wrath, strife, sedition's, heresies, envying, murder, drunkenness, reveling, and such like are totally unproductive to God. They are lifeless, degenerating, and lead to eternal damnation. Other scriptural references of dead works include Romans 1:18-2:3; 1 Corinthians 6:9-10; Revelation 21:8.

Overview of Dead Works

1. Sin: the open rejection and disobedience of God's word.
2. Religious practices that do not bring reconciliation to God and are the product our self-will.
3. Works of the flesh, actions that are the product of a fallen, depraved, and sinful nature.

It is fundamental that before one will repent, they must first be condemned and come to know they are wrong and out of step with God. They must hear something. What? The gospel delivered by God's messengers, the ministry.

> *For whosoever shall call upon the name of the Lord shall be saved. How then shall they call on him in whom they have not believed? And how shall they believe in him of whom they have not heard? And how shall they hear without a preacher - Faith comes by hearing, and hearing by the word of God (Romans 10:13-17).*

To hear the message that condemns is not enough. The message must be believed in the heart and obeyed.

Necessity for Repentance

Man needs to repent in an effort to reverse the death sentence imposed on him from the garden of Eden (Genesis 3). God imposed the sentence of damnation and only he can reverse it (Mark 2:5-11). Repentance is man's proof of sincerity and desire to please, and serve God. To repent our ways and live in God's way is an acknowledgment that man's ways are wrong and God's way is right.

Repentance is a demand from God, *"and at the time of this ignorance God winked at; but now commandeth all men everywhere to repent"* (Acts 17:30). There is no way man can hide from God or escape the judgment of God until he repents (Job 34:21-23). Man needs to repent in order to obtain eternal life and not suffer eternal damnation. God threatens to judge man, but conditions the threat by opening a door of escape through offering a reprieve,

> *I will judge you, O house of Israel, everyone according to your ways, saith the Lord God. Repent, and turn yourselves from all your transgressions; so iniquity shall not be your ruin, why will you die O house of Israel For I have no pleasure in the death of him that dieth, saith the Lord God;*

wherefore turn yourselves and live (Ezekiel 18:23; 18:30-32; 2 Peter 3:9).

Attitudes that Prompt Repentance

"The sacrifices of God are a broken spirit: a broken and contrite heart, O God, thou wilt not despise" (Psalms 51:17; 34:18; Isaiah 66:2). Part of man's nature is to justify himself in an effort to minimize his wrongdoing. When a man is honest before God, he will acknowledge his guiltiness and glorify God's righteousness. The attitude is, 'Lord, I deserve whatever comes my way, but let your mercy and grace lift me out of my condition. Many show sorrow over their transgressions because they were caught and not necessarily because they are remorseful for wrongdoing. The self-justifying spirit must be broken, then humbled in the presence of God. David's attitude expressed in the Book of Psalms (51:3-4) is an example of the attitude every repenting sinner must imitate.

> *For I acknowledge my transgressions: and my sin is ever before me. Against thee, thee only, have I sinned, and done this evil in thy sight: that thou mightest be justified when thou speakest, and be clear when thou judgest.*

The one important attitude that will impress God is one's readiness to stop sinning (Psalm 38:17). Until one is ready to forsake their ways, there is no reconciliation with God. One of the best examples of the difference between self-justification and repentance is illustrated in the Book of Luke (18:9-14). While praying in the temple, a Pharisee reminded God of his good deeds and showcased his exemplary conducts whereas, the Pharisee's neighbor, the publican, had a different attitude toward God.

> *And the publican, standing afar off, would not lift so much as his eyes to heaven, but smote upon his breast, saying, God be merciful unto me a sinner. [Jesus responded] I tell you, this man went down to his house justified rather than the other: for everyone that exalteth himself shall be abased, and he that humbleth himself shall be exalted (vs 13-14).*

The great lesson of humility is driven home and anyone who really wants a relationship with Christ must descend from their mountain of self-justification and contritely kneel at the feet of Jesus.

Examples of Repentance

One of the examples of repentance found in the Old Testament is in the Book of Jonah. When the King of Ninevehand and the people heard the prophet Jonah preached a short message five things happened:

1. They **heard** the message or they gave earnest heed to it.
2. They **believed** the message. To them, it was a true message and published it abroad.
3. They **acted** on the message by humbling themselves with fasting and sackcloth.
4. They **cried** out to God for mercy and help.
5. They **turned** from their evil way.

When God saw their actions and recognized that they truly repented, He changed His mind by giving the city a reprieve (Jonah 3:4-10). One of the best New Testament examples is found in the Book of Luke (15:4-32). When the young man came to himself and was the key that changed his direction in life. It was not until he was stripped of all his resources and self-respect that he saw the futility of his lifestyle then, he was ready to stop.

He did not return home proud and arrogant but humbled and unworthy to be called his father's son.

Condition of Repentance

Before repentance can be reached man's condition must be revealed. Man's condition? The universal condition of all men is depravity, deceitfulness, and desperate wickedness (Jeremiah 17:9). *"The way of man is not in himself: it is not in man to direct his own steps"* (Jeremiah 10:23). *"There is none righteous, no, not one"* and *"All have sinned and come short of the glory of God"* (Romans 3:10; 23). These Scriptures and many others illustrate the condition of man and the need to repent. Since man does not have the ability to help himself in that regard nor assist his brother, he must turn to the only one who can deliver from the dilemma of sin. Society has developed social programs and invented self-help methods which may work to change actions, but cannot change human nature. Only Jesus Christ can change the nature of man from evil to good. The Book of Titus describes the transformation of the condition of man (3:3-8). The past is the dead works while the new life is one of the good works, which is pleasing to God. Before one seeks out eternal life they must first realize they are dead and need to be spiritually resurrected.

Human mortality has three stages: the first stage is spiritual separation from God. When Adam ate the fruit of the forbidden tree he experienced separation from God. The initial experience did not immediately have an impact on his body but his sin severed his relationship with his Creator. As a result of Adam's sin, humanity inherited a sinful condition, *"dead in trespasses and sins"* (Ephesians 2:1-3). He will remain spiritually dead until awakened by the life that comes from Christ. The life one lives in sin is filled with 'dead works' (Hebrews 9:14). Turning toward eternal life requires one to turn from sin. The second stage of death is the grave when the body surrenders to the spirit that made it active. The last and final stage is eternal judgment and the damnation of Hell. The Book of Revelation terms this stage as the "second death" (Revelation 20:14).

The motions of sin are sinful actions prompted by a sinful nature (Romans 7:5-14). While living in sin, one is free from righteousness. Our righteousness is as filthy and worthless before God (Isaiah 64:6; Romans 6:12-22).

The Fruit of Repentance

John the Baptist stated during the days of his ministry, *"bring forth fruit worthy of repentance"* (Matthew 3). What is the fruit to be produced? The new converts in the Book of Acts destroyed all their sinful items (19:18-19). If one has truly turned away from sin, the tools of sin are no longer needed. To keep them around is to face temptation that one may not be able to master. For instance, pour the alcohol down the drain, throw the cartons of tobacco into the fire, pick up your clothes and leave the sweetheart's house, leave the dens of iniquity, and straighten up your act. A repented heart expresses itself in this manner, *"I abhor myself"* (Job 42:6) and *"I will not justify myself"* (Job 9:20). This is one fruit of repentance many find difficult to produce because naturally it's easier to blame others than to take ownership of wrongdoing.

Forsaking one's sinful ways is a sign of repentance provided it is more than cosmetics. To cease from an activity without changing the attitude toward it opens the door to return to the former ways. See Isaiah 55:7; Joel 2:12-13; 1 Kings 8:47-48 as additional references. One final sign of repentance is the willingness to be instructed through Scripture. If one is confronted with their errors but refuses to receive instruction or admonition, then repentance is very shallow or non-existent. *"Surely after I was turned, I repented; and after that, I was instructed, I smote upon my thigh: I was ashamed, yea, even confounded, because I did bear the reproach of my youth* (Jeremiah 31:18-19; Psalms 38:3).

Additional References

- Acts 19:18-19: the new believers got rid of all their sinful items.
- Job. 42:6: I abhor myself.
- Job. 9:20: I will not justify myself.
- I Kings 8:47-48: repent and turn to God with all your heart.
- Isaiah 55:7: let the wicked forsake his way.
- Jonah 3:10: what repentance will do?
- Jeremiah 31:18-19: to repent was instructed.
- Joel 2:12-13: lend your hearts and not your garments.
- Psalms 38:3: I will declare my iniquity and be sorry for my sins.

Signs of Repentance

Listed below are a few of the signs that go along with a truly repentant heart:

- Sorrow, anguish, remorse, contriteness, and shame.
- A bitter hatred and disgust of one's past conduct.
- Humility.
- Complete forsaking.
- Pursuant to do the right thing.
- An attitude to be instructed.
- Honesty and not self-justification or excuses.
- Avoid the environment of misconduct.
- Submissive and obedience.

- Belief put into action.

God's Methods for Repentance

God uses three common ways to persuade men to repent. The first, the honey method is found in the Book of Romans, *"or despiseth thou the riches of his goodness and forbearance and long suffering; not know that the goodness of God leadeth to repentance"* (2:4). God knows the weakness of man; hence, he exercises long-suffering providing a time span for man to repent (Psalms 130:3-4; 103:11-14). He is filled with mercy, ready to forgive, which expresses His goodness toward man, encouraging him to repent (Psalm 86:5). To fear Him is to acknowledge that He is right and the repentant sinner is willing to surrender to God's will. Man does so by confessing his sin or admitting that he is a sinner. Fear is giving reverence and honor to God.

The second, the stick method, can be seen in Job 33:14-30:

> *In a dream, in a vision of night. He opens the ear of men that he may withdraw man from his purpose [turn him around] and hide pride from man - he is chastened also with **pain** upon his bed and the multitude of his bones with **strong pain**.*

God lays on man the burden of adversity, trouble, and suffering to get him to see the error of his ways. Many persons have gone through much agony before they were willing to repent. "He looketh upon men, and if any say, I have sinned and perverted that which is right, and it profited me not; he will deliver his soul from going into the pit [hell] (vs. 27-30).

A third method is pleading and persuasion,

> *Wash you, make you clean, put away the evil of your doings from before mine eyes; cease to do evil; learn to do well. Come now, let us **reason** together saith the Lord; Though*

your sins be as scarlet, they shall be white as snow. If you be willing and obedient, ye shall eat the good of the land (Isaiah 1:16-20).

God uses the ministry to preach the Gospel to all men as demonstrated in the final face-to-face message that Jesus left the Apostolic fathers, *"that repentance and remission of sin should be preached in **his name**"* (Luke 24:47). Repentance is a real change of mind and attitude toward sin which effectuates total change of life conduct and relationship before God. Repentance is not just regret or remorse. When one repents, they turn to God to do His commandments.

Paul's defense before King Agrippa was his commission from Jesus Christ to preach the Gospel to the Gentiles, *"That they should repent and turn to God [from idols] and do works meet for repentance"* (Acts 26:20; 1 Thessalonians 1:9). One is not ready to be baptized until they have fully believed and repented of their sin and are ready to turn to serve God before whom they express faith in.

Having taken the first step, Repentance from Dead Works, one is now ready for the next step on the staircase of the *Six Principles of the Doctrine of Christ*, **faith toward God.**

PRINCIPLE II

~2~
FAITH TOWARD GOD

Faith cometh by hearing, and hearing by the word of God.

--Romans 10:17

The next step up the staircase is faith toward God. Notice it is not faith in God, but faith toward God. Since repentance is the changing of the mind, faith toward God is turning to Him, whom we expect to receive cleansing, forgiveness, and the fulfillment of His promises. Please note the difference between faith in God and faith toward God. Faith in God is to have confidence in His ability and the truthfulness of His Word. Faith toward God is to expect something from God, that which we believe in. It is to believe that God is and is a rewarder of those who seek Him (Hebrews 11:6). After repentance, one turns to God for deliverance. Faith in God is to believe in God. Faith toward God is to expect to receive the things God has promised.

Faith is the expectancy that one has to receive something from God (forgiveness of sins, the power to live above sin), a faith that is rooted and established in God only. The gospel directs us to Jesus from whom we are to receive this expectancy. (Note: Acts 3:19; Acts 5:31; Acts 10:43; Acts 13:38; Acts 26:18).

Belief is to accept someone or something (God's word) as being true and trustworthy. To be persuaded or convinced by the testimony of things not observed.

Faith must have an object. It is not some abstract belief gathered from the imagination but is based on the Word of God. The object of faith is Jesus Christ. It is to Him one looks to receive the promises made by God. Faith toward God in this section is not expecting the Holy Ghost as a primary focus, but the promise of the remission of sin, and a clear record by virtue of the shed blood of Jesus the sacrificial Lamb of God. The purpose for Jesus coming into the world was to *"save his people from their sins"* (Matthew 1:21). Jesus taught that *"Except you believe that I am he, ye shall die in your sins"* (John 8:24). True repentance is the expectation of the remission of sins. This forgiveness comes through the blood of Jesus. Without the shedding of His blood, there is no remission of sins (Hebrews 9:22).

Day of Atonement

Israel's annual Day of Atonement was a spiritual cleansing that came in the fall of every year, six months after the celebration of the Passover. According to the Jewish calendar, it came on the tenth day of the seventh month (Leviticus 23:26-32; Numbers 29:7-11). Unlike the other Jewish holidays, the Day of Atonement was no festive event. It was a day of national mourning and repentance. This was a Sabbath Day celebration, which meant that no work could be done (Leviticus 23:26-32). Anyone who did not observe this Sabbath was to be cut off from His people (Leviticus 23:29), which is a euphemism for being put to death. The day was a time of humility for all Israel (Leviticus 16:31; 23:27; Numbers 29:7) and it included fasting.

This would thus be the only religious holiday which was characterized by mourning, fasting, and repentance.

The Old Testament system of sacrificing bulls, goats, and lambs did not remove sin, but only covered a temporary solution until the real sacrifice, Jesus the Lamb of God, came on the scene (Hebrews 10:4). On the Day of Atonement, the eyes of all Israel were on the ruling high priest as he entered into the holy of holies with the blood of the goat to obtain an atonement for their sins. Once every year the high priest had to go through the same procedure and Israel's expectation or faith was toward God who gave them a reprieve for another year. The high priest for the New Testament church is Jesus Christ. He entered once into the holy place-Heaven; carrying His own blood as the sacrificial Lamb of God, then presented it to Himself as God and was satisfied. The price has been paid for all mankind and it is now man's responsibility to have faith in this blood to receive forgiveness of sins. It is the blood of Jesus that purges one's conscience from dead works (Isaiah 53:10-11; Hebrews 10:8-13). The sacrificial plan was devised by God, not as an emergency solution for an unexpected event in the Garden of Eden, but a planned remedy for the fall of man before it transpired. The remedy was in place before the foundation of the world because Jesus was the Lamb slain "before the foundation of the world" (1 Peter 18-21; Revelation 5:9; 13:8).

Faith toward God is to expect something from Him. What is one to expect? Forgiveness and remission of sin. One must look to Jesus and the blood He shed and have faith in Him. Faith toward God is looking to Jesus Christ for redemption. Israel was looking for their Messiah, but with the wrong purpose. They expected a restored kingdom (Act 1:6). Since Jesus did not bring that hope, their faith in Christ was destroyed. If they had only known the purpose of the Messiah to provide a way for sins to be remitted they would not have rejected Him as a nation. If one does not set their faith in Jesus now, all other efforts to be saved will be in vain.

Peter's sermon before Cornelius pointed him toward Jesus by directing his faith toward Lord for the remission of sins.

Cornelius believed the message to be true and his expectation was to receive from Jesus the promise Peter declared was his to have (Acts 10:43). Furthermore, Apostle Paul preached to the Jews and Gentiles,

> *That through this man (Jesus) is preached unto you the forgiveness of sins and by him, all that believe are justified from all things, from which ye could not be justified by the law of Moses"* (Acts 13:38-39).

Again, faith toward God is focused on Jesus.

> *Man is not justified by the works of the law (dead works) but by the faith of Jesus Christ, even we have believed in Jesus Christ, that we might be justified by the faith of Christ, and not by the works of the law: For by the works of the law shall no flesh be justified (Galatians 2:16).*

What is the expectancy? Justification! Justification is the privilege to stand in God's presence without being rejected. How can this be? It must be through faith in Jesus Christ and the price paid for man's guilt of sin. *"Wherein he hath made us accepted in the beloved. In whom we have redemption through his blood, the forgiveness of sins, according to the riches of his grace"* (Ephesians 1:6-7). See also Colossians 1:13-14. How is one accepted before God? By faith toward Jesus Christ. *"Testifying both to the Jews, and also to the Greeks, repentance toward God, and faith toward our Lord Jesus Christ"* (Acts 20:21). Reconciliation and peace with God are made possible by the shed blood on the cross. Man who was estranged and separated from God, even his enemy, can now be reconciled with Him through the sacrificial work of Jesus on the cross at Calvary.

It is God's design that one believes in Him through His Son. The Scripture says, *"Who being in the brightness of his glory, and **the express image of his person**, and upholding all things by the word of his power, when he himself purged our sins, sat down on the right hand of the Majesty on high"* (Hebrews 1:3).

Jesus sat down, indicating His work was finished. All that remains is for one to exercise faith toward God through Jesus.

Scriptural References on Faith Toward God

- Galatians 3:22: All under sin, but the promise is given to those that believe.
- Hebrews 11:6: Believe God, He is a rewarder of those that seek Him.
- Romans 10:13-20: How can they call on Him whom they do not know exists?
- Acts 20:21: Faith toward the Lord Jesus Christ.
- Acts 14:15; 14:27: The door of faith opened to the Gentiles. How? The gospel is preached to them.
- Acts 15:7-11: Purified their hearts by faith, gave the Holy Ghost.
- Hebrews 10:22: A heart in full assurance of faith.
- Acts 26:18: Turn men from the power of Satan toward God.
- Isaiah 40:3; Malachi 3:1; Malachi 4:6; Luke 1:16: Whose responsibility was to introduce Jesus to Israel.
- Matthews 8:5-10: Not found this faith in Israel. He expected something by action.
- Romans 3:20-27: Justified by faith in Jesus Christ.
- Romans 10:2-3: They trusted (Israel) in themselves, and not God.
- Titus 2:10: Showing all good fidelity (faith).

The preaching of the gospel is the key to faith toward God. It points our expectancy to Jesus Christ who did the will of God for our deliverance. Having confidence in God through Jesus Christ because we believe God's word to be trustworthy and we look for something from Him.

Faith must have an object on which to focus and that object is Jesus Christ.
1. His shed blood on Calvary.
2. His words.
3. His works.
4. The Holy Scriptures.

Note these additional support scriptural references: Galatians 2:6; Ephesians 3:12; Philippians 3:9.

We hear something to believe and when we believe what we heard, we expect to receive it on the evidence of what we have heard.

- Romans 4:19-21: Abraham not weak in faith expected something.
- Galatians 1:23-25: The law was a schoolmaster to bring the Jews to Christ.

Christ, who is the object of our faith, eliminates any further need for the ordinances of the Law to be practiced. He requires just faith in the plan he has established through Christ. One is not ready for water baptism until they have a knowledge of whom we look toward for forgiveness.

Now that Faith Toward God has been established one is ready for the next step on this ascending staircase, the Doctrine of Baptisms.

PRINCIPLE III

~3~
DOCTRINE OF BAPTISMS

There is also an antitype which now saves us; baptism (not the removal of the filth of the flesh, but the answer of a good conscience toward God), through the resurrection of Jesus Christ.

--1 Peter 3:21

The doctrine and practice of baptism is one of the most misunderstood tenets of Christianity in the modern church age. In the *Greek-English Lexicon of the New Testament,* the word "baptize" originated from the Greek term, "baptize in" or "baptizo", which means to fully immerse, to be soaked in, to put beneath, or submersion in water. Its symbol of use in the Old Testament is cleansing, typified by the brass laver of water before the tabernacle and temple. The purpose of baptism is clearly stated in the Scriptures when Peter instructed those gathered with him to be baptized in the **name of Jesus Christ for the remission of sins** (Acts 2:38). The New Testament practice of baptism was always in a body of water to be entered into, and never implies a sprinkling of water from a dish, bowl, or decanter. John 3:23, states that John the Baptist performed water baptisms in Aenon because there was and abundance of water at that location or "much water there".

When one has manifested faith toward God, the expectancy is to receive the remission of sins (Colossians 1:4; 2:11-14). Baptism is commanded by God (Mark 16:16; John 3:3-5; Acts 2:38; Matthew 28:19). Baptism is like the burial of someone that passes from one life to the next. We are buried in baptism as one that is dead to sin and are resurrected to live a new lifestyle (Romans 6:3-6; 1 Corinthians 15:29). It is a washing process to remove past sins from one's life as referenced in Acts 2:38.

The Scriptures speak of the doctrine of baptisms, plural, there must be more than one baptism to be applied. There is water baptism and spirit baptism. Jesus speaks of being born of water and spirit without such experience one cannot discover nor enter into the Kingdom of God (John 3:3-5). John the Baptist states, he baptized with water, but there is one coming after who will baptize with the Holy Ghost and fire (Luke 3:16). Furthermore, Jesus instructed the disciples to go to Jerusalem until they are baptized with the Holy Ghost; the promise of the Father (Acts 1:5). To be baptized in water in the Name of Jesus and filled with the Holy Ghost constitutes the two parts of the new birth experience: water and spirit, making one baptism. The Scriptures speak of **one Lord, one faith,** and **one baptism**, but this one baptism is in two parts (Ephesians 4:4-6). Another supporting Scripture about the new birth experience is noted by the washing of regeneration and renewing of the Holy Ghost (Titus 3:5-6).

In John 3:25-26, a dispute arose between John the Baptist's disciples and certain Jews over the issue of ceremonial washing or purification. The Jews had a number of ritual washings and they accused the disciples of Jesus for not washing before dining. The act of washing for consecration or for purification from uncleanness involved washing all or part of the body, or one's clothing. Jesus Christ's attitude to the Pharisees reflected, not a disavowal of ritual washing, but disapproval of their emphasis on the outward, rather than inward forms of religion (Matthew 15:1-11).

Purification is the process by which an unclean person, according to the Levitical Law thereby cut off from the sanctuary and the festivals, was restored to the enjoyment of all these privileges. The great annual purification of the Jews was on the Day of Atonement. Purification and washings were established in the law of Moses and were typical of washing to cleanse one of all the impurities before serving in the tabernacle (Numbers 8:5-7, 21). The Levites were to be sprinkled and washed to make themselves clean. For instance, before the high priest Aaron and his sons could go into the sanctuary, they had to wash themselves at the brazen laver of water standing before the tabernacle. More than washing was necessary for Aaron and his sons. They also had to be anointed with the holy anointing oil before entering the tabernacle. If they did not, they were to die, symbolizing the necessity of our washing and cleansing by water baptism and anointing (filled) with the Holy Ghost before we can enter into the sanctuary, the Church.

The Purpose of Baptism Is Washing or Cleansing

- Exodus 29:4: Aaron and sons brought before the door of the tabernacle and washed.
- Exodus 30:17-21: The Laver for Aaron and sons to wash.
- Hebrews 9:9-14: The practice of the Law; washing and purification.
- Acts 22:16: Arise and be baptized, washing away thy sins.
- Titus 3:5: The washing of regeneration. Regeneration is to be formed again; new birth.
- 1 Corinthians 6:11: Now you are washed by baptism and set free.

Old Testament Sense of Spiritual Baptisms

- Psalm 26:6; 51:2; 51:7: Wash from my iniquity, purge me with hyssop.
- Isaiah 1:6: Wash you, make you clean, put away the evil of your doings.
- Jeremiah 4:4: Wash thine heart from wickedness.
- Zechariah 13:1: A fountain opened for sin and uncleanness.
- Ezekiel 36:25: God to sprinkle clean water on you to be clean.
- Leviticus 15:12: Washed from defilement (vs 5-6).
- 2 Kings 5:10-14: Naaman, go wash.

Scriptures on Water Baptism

- Mark 1: 4-5: John's baptism unto repentance.
- Galatians 3: 27: Baptized into Christ, have put on Christ.
- Romans 6:3-4: Baptized into Christ.
- I Peter 3:21: Baptism an answer of a good conscience.
- Ephesians 5:26: Washing of water by (according) to the word. (See Hebrews 10:22).
- 1 Corinthians 12:13: Baptized into one body.
- Acts 8:12-16; 36-37: When they believed the preaching of Philip, they were baptized.

Link Between Baptism and Circumcision

- Acts 2:38: Be baptized for the remission of sin.
- Colossians 2:10-13: Circumcision made without hands.
- Romans 2:28-29: The circumcision of the heart.
- Jeremiah 4:4: Take away the foreskin on the heart.

- Deuteronomy 30:6: The Lord will circumcise the heart.

Note: Acts 19:1-6; Acts 16:14-15: Where belief and faith are the prime factors.

Baptism Is Not Optional It Is a Command

- Mark 16:16: He that believeth and is baptized shall be saved.
- Acts 10:48: Peter commanded Cornelius and his house to be baptized.
- Matthew 28:19: Baptism in name of Father, Son, Holy Ghost-these are titles. The name is JESUS.
- Acts 22:16: Arise and be baptized, washing away thy sins.
- John 3:3-5: You must be born of water and spirit.

The Blood of Christ Combined with Faith and Water Baptism Completes the Cleansing Process

- Revelation 1:5: He washed us from sin in His own blood.
- John 1:7: The blood of Jesus cleanses us from all sin.
- John 5:7-8: There are three that bear witness in earth; Spirit, water, and blood.

The "Name" and "Blood" Are One

- Acts 4:10; 4:12: There is salvation in no other name but Jesus.
- Acts 5:28: You have used His **name** to bring His blood on us.
- Acts 10:36; 10:43: Through His name, you shall receive remission of sins.
- Acts 8:12: When they believed Philip, they were baptized in the **name** of Jesus.

- Acts 18:8: Many Corinthians believed and were baptized in the name.

The Importance of Using the Name of Jesus

The **name of Jesus** alone has the power and authority to remove sin from our lives! One cannot accept Christ without fully accepting His name, Jesus. It is in the name, "JESUS", that all power and authority resides. The **name** represents the person.

- Luke 5:20-24: Son of man has the power to forgive sins.
- Mark 2:7; 2:10; Luke 7:49; Jeremiah 31:31-34
- Luke 24:46-47: Repentance and remission of sins preached in His name.
- Acts 4:10-12: Salvation in no other name but Jesus (v.18).
- Acts 2:38: Baptize in the **name of the Lord Jesus Christ**.
- Colossians 3:17: In all you do in word or deed, do in the name of Jesus.
- Acts 10:36; 10:43: Preach peace and through His name receive remission of sins.
- John 20:31: We have life through His name.
- Acts 8:12; 8:16: When they believed they were baptized in the name of Jesus.
- Acts 10:48: Commanded to be baptized in the name of Jesus.
- Acts 19:5: When they heard this they were baptized in the name of Jesus.
- Acts 22:16: Arise, wash away thy sins, calling on the name of the Lord (Jesus).

- Matthew 28:19: Baptize in the name (singular) of the Father, Son, and Holy Ghost.

    The name of the Father is **Jesus** (John 5:43).

    The name of the Son is **Jesus** (Luke 1: 31; Matthew 1: 21).

    The name of the Holy Ghost is **Jesus** (John 14: 26).

In my experience as a pastor, most Christian persecutions arise from the use of the **name of Jesus** and not necessarily the use of the word **God**. See Acts 4:18; Acts 4:2-31; 5:28; 5:40; 1 Peter 4:14. To baptize in the name is synonymous with being baptized **into** the name. Thus becoming the property of the one whose name was used.

- Acts 3:6; 3:16: Through faith in His name was this man healed.
- Matthew 28:18: All authority in Heaven and earth belongs to Jesus.
- Colossians 1:15-17: By Jesus were all things created.

Responsibilities to Use the Name

- 2 Timothy 2:19: Everyone who utters the name of Christ, is to depart from evil.
- Galatians 3:27: When you are baptized into Christ, you have put on Christ.
- John 1:12: Power to become the sons of God; believe in **His name**.
- Acts 4:30: Do signs and wonders in the **name** of **Jesus**.
- Exodus 3:13-14: Moses asked what is thy name? Say, I AM, sent you.
- John 8:58: Jesus said, before Abraham was, I WAS.
- Judges 13:18: Why ask my name seeing it's a secret.

- Isaiah 9:6: His name is called Wonderful, Everlasting Father, etc...
- Matthew 12:21: In His name shall the Gentiles trust.
- Matthew 1:21: The name revealed-call His name **Jesus** (Luke 1:31)
- Matthew 1:23: Call His name Emmanuel, God with us (Isaiah 7:14).
- John 5:23; 5:28: Honor son as the Father.
- I John 2:23: He that acknowledgeth the Son has the Father also.
- John 10:30: I and my Father are one.
- 2 Corinthians 5:19: God in Christ reconciling the world to Himself
- I Timothy 3:16: God was manifested in the world.
- John 14:7-10: He that has seen me has seen the Father.
- John 12:44-45: See me see Him that sent me.
- Philippians 2:9-11: Jesus given a name above every name.
- Proverbs 18:10: Name of Lord a strong tower.
- John 14:13-14; John 15:16; John 16:23-26: When you ask in **my name** it shall be done for you.

~4~
HOW WERE YOU BAPTIZED?

Repentance and remission of sins should be preached in his name among all nations, beginning at Jerusalem.

--Luke 24:47

The question regarding the mode of baptism is as old as the church and the correct mode is so important to the salvation and eternal life of mankind. Although I classify myself as a Christian, the answer to the appropriate mode of baptism becomes all the more important unless I have believed the gospel in vain. Apostle Paul found some disciples in Ephesus and began to question them about their faith:

> *Have ye received the Holy Ghost since ye believed? And they said unto him, We have not so much as heard whether there be any Holy Ghost. And he said Unto them, unto what then were ye baptized? And they said, Unto John's baptism* (Acts 19:1-3).

In my years of pastoring, most Christians profess in varying degrees the necessity of baptism but are not able to agree as to how or the purpose of baptism. Let us examine a few reasons in an effort to find out "unto what were you baptized", and see if that baptism agrees with our guidebook, the Bible. Some believe baptism is about identifying with a particular church or religious organizations by making themselves subject to a set of rules or form of doctrine formulated and established by their associated religious organization. Ultimately, their basic intention is to obtain membership in the church of their choice. Other Christians claim they were baptized to associate with the faith of their mother, father, or some other loved ones. They have no real conviction of their own but trust that what was good enough for their mother or father is good enough for them. They feel justified and very satisfied to please men, but little thought as to what God might require. These persons' basic purpose is to continue in their family religious tradition. Another group believes baptism to be an outward show of an inward work or a sign to other people that they belong to Christ, an accepted child to live a Christian life. Their objective is to prove to others their faith and belief in Jesus Christ. Some were baptized simply to be called a Christian, being unconcerned about the method used, supposing any baptism will suffice. The end goal is to be called a Christian and to remove the shame of being called a non-believer.

Others were baptized as babies, small children, or adults as an entrance into the Christian faith. Many, in all honesty, desire to serve the Lord, to truly identified with Christ, and be ready for the appearance of Jesus when he returns for His bride, the church (Revelations 21:9). They do not know for sure which way to go or which mode of baptism to accept but are doing the best they know and are living according to all the knowledge that has come across their pathway. Since these individuals do not know the way according to the Scriptures, they are dependent on others to guide them and if their guides are wrong, then they will be misled. It was to such a group Apostle Paul addressed. They sought to do right and were living according to all the knowledge they have obtained, but something was still lacking. The previous baptism they had became outdated because the one John the Baptist shared with them has become obsolete since the beginning of the ministry of Jesus Christ. When Jesus began His ministry he introduced a new era of salvation.

Before you proceed with the reading, re-evaluate your baptism. Does any of the above mentioned applies to you? Are you lacking the Holy Spirit as the Ephesian believers that encountered Paul? Let us examine the Holy Bible to determine the purpose of baptism. Specifically, the necessity of baptism, the method, and its administration? When Apostle Paul asked the Ephesian disciples regarding their baptism, they answered,

*Unto John's baptism. Then said Paul, John verily baptized with the baptism of repentance, saying unto the people, that they should believe on him, which should come after him, that is, in Christ Jesus. When they heard this, they were baptized in the **name of the Lord Jesus*** (Acts 19:3-5).

For them to believe in Christ required them to perform the directive of the Word of God and to be immersed in His name by baptism. Simply to be called a 'believer' does not identify one with Christ, but a true believer is one who will continue in the teaching or doctrine of Jesus Christ. They are not simply hearers of His Word but doers also and keep all of His commandments. *"Jesus said unto those Jews which believed on him, If ye continue in my word, then are ye my disciples indeed"* (John 8:31; Matthew 7:24; 7:25; James 1:22-25). Again Jesus said, *"And why call ye me, Lord, Lord, and do not the things which I say?"* (Luke 6:46). To believe on Jesus Christ as the Scriptures declare is the first step toward baptism. *"He that cometh to God must first believe that he is, and also that he is a rewarder of them that diligently seek him"* (Hebrews 11:6; Mark 16:16).

Peter gives us the exact formula and purpose for baptism in the Book of Acts 2:38, *"Then Peter said unto them, repent, and be baptized every one of you in the name of Jesus Christ, for the remission of sins, and ye shall receive the gift of the Holy Ghost"*. This reply was made in response to the cry "men and brethren" what shall we do? (v 37), in other words, how can we be saved? Let us examine Peter's answer.

The first directive is to **repent**. To be baptized without repentance would be likened to a person trying to wash themselves while yet handling the things that has made them dirty in the first place. Repentance is a changing or turning away, in your heart and mind, from the practice of all sin and ungodliness. It is not simply just being sorry and shedding a few tears, then returning to the same sinful practices. True repentance makes one sorrowful and it will produce hatred, abhorrence, and a complete shamefulness for all manner and practice of sin and evil works. One must develop a sincere desire to completely change or turn away from these things and ask God, Lord, if you will forgive and deliver me from the power of sin and cleanse me completely, I will never return to these sinful practices again. This process alone is not salvation, but a preparation for baptism. It really saddens me as a pastor that many individuals stop here in this juncture of the salvation process. Repentance is but a preparation for one to be baptized (Ezekiel 18:20-21; 18:30-31; Isaiah 55:7; Isaiah 1:16; Acts 3:19). Which alludes to the question, how could a baby who is a few days old or a very young child repent from sin when they have no knowledge in such matters?

Apostle Peter tells us that baptism is an answer of a good conscience toward God (Peter 3:20-21). The only way we can have a good conscience is to be void of any offense before God, washed and have forsaken all practices of sin and evil. To walk before Him pure and spotless. The only way this can be accomplished is to be washed and have the stain of sin removed so that we might walk in the newness of life, honest, and free before Him unto all well pleasing (Isaiah 1:18; Romans 6:1-7; Galatians 3: 27; Colossians 1:10; 2:14). Furthermore, a good conscience is to be free from a guilty conscience. A condition that God can judge and the individual be found guiltless because their sins have been remitted and are not held to their account anymore (Ezekiel 18:21-22).

The next instruction of Peter is to be baptized in the *name of Jesus Christ for the remission of sins*. It is in the water of baptism that the blood of Christ, which was shed for us, washes and completely remove or cleanses us of all sin, *"and the blood of Jesus Christ his Son cleanseth us from all sin"* (I John 1:7; 5:6-

8). Therefore the primary purpose of baptism is to wash away sin and make the believer clean. Our baptism must not only be accompanied by repentance but also by faith, believing that our sins are remitted or removed once and for all. Scripture says, *"And their sins and iniquities will I remember no more"* (Hebrews 10:17; Psalm 3:11-12).

It is very important to emphasize that water baptism is only valid or effective when the proper authority or name is invoked. The name is **Jesus Christ**. Because He alone is able to save or remit our sins. This was His purpose in coming to give His life and shed His blood, blotting out our sins and transgressions, thus making us free. There is salvation in no other name but in the name of Jesus (Acts 4:7-12; John 8:32-36). Consider the following Scripture concerning biblical examples of baptism. Philip preached Jesus Christ in Samaria and they received his teaching and were baptized but they have not as yet received the Holy Ghost. The Scriptures say *"for as yet he [the Holy Ghost] was fallen upon none of them; only they were baptized in the name of Jesus"*(Acts 8:12-17).

Peter went to Caesarea to the house of one named Cornelius to declare unto him and his household the word of God. After having believed Peter's speaking, the Holy Ghost fell on all them which heard the word.

> *For they heard them speak with tongues and magnify God. Then answered Peter, Can any man forbid water, that these should not be baptized, which have received the Holy Ghost as well as we? And he commanded them to be baptized in the name of the Lord* [Jesus Christ] (Acts 10:46-48).

Paul taught certain disciples at Ephesus about baptism in the name of Jesus, *"when they heard this, they were baptized in the name of the Lord Jesus"* (Acts 19:5). Later, Paul testifying of his conversion, spoke of Ananias as he came to him, *"And now why tarriest thou? Arise, and be baptized, and wash away thy sins, calling on the name of the Lord"* (Acts 22:16). Ultimately, the name of the Lord is revealed as Jesus (Acts 9:17).

There is one thing in common with all the Scriptures mentioned above, all were baptized in the name of Jesus (Acts 2:38; 8:16; 10:48; 19:5; 22:16). The Scriptures say, out of the mouth of two or three witnesses, every word of God shall be established (Matthew 18:16). In these writings, we have four witnesses: Peter, Philip, Paul, and Ananias. These witnesses are each saying the same thing to three groups of people: the Jews, the Samaritan, and the Gentiles. Baptism must be performed in the **name of Jesus.**

One may ask, what did Jesus mean when He said to baptize in the name of the Father, and of the Son, and of the Holy Ghost? This is found in Matthew 28:19, *"Go ye therefore, and teach all nations, baptizing them in the name of the Father, and of the Son, and of the Holy Ghost"*. Jesus did not say use the titles, Father, Son, and Holy Ghost, but rather used the name of the one to whom these titles apply. In verse 18, Jesus said, *"All power is given unto me in heaven and in earth"*. The *Greek-English Lexicon of the New Testament* translates the term "power" to authority, and it is in Him (Jesus) that the authority rests to baptize. To do what Jesus taught one must first know the right name to use. What is the name of the Father, the Son, and the Holy Ghost? John 5:43 states, *"I [Jesus] come in my Father's name, and ye received me not: if another shall come in his own name, him ye will receive"*. Luke 1:31-32 says,*"And, behold, thou shalt conceive in thy womb and bring forth a son, and shalt call his name Jesus. He shall be great, and be called the 'Son of the Highest'"*. Also see Matthew 1:21. Apostle John shared in his writing, *"But the Comforter, which is the Holy Ghost, whom the Father will send in my name [Jesus], he shall teach all things, and bring all things to your remembrance whatsoever I have said unto you"* (John 14:26).

Saint Luke records the same words of Jesus in a parallel manner, *"And that repentance and remission of sins should be preached in his name among all nations, beginning at Jerusalem"* (Luke 24:47). This is not a different saying of Jesus, but the same words, amplified and explained to our understanding. As a capstone, Paul sums up the matter, *"And whatsoever ye do in word or deed, do all in the name of the Lord Jesus, giving thanks to God and the Father by him"* (Colossians 3:17). This includes baptism as well.

Read and consider what is written and may the Lord give you the understanding because it is the foundation of the New Testament salvation era. There is but one Lord, one faith, and one baptism (Ephesians 4:5). Baptism is not left up to one's interpretation, seeing there is but one, therefore, that one must be performed according to the Scriptures in the name of Jesus.

Another point to consider, how should baptism be performed? Is it in water by immersion, sprinkling, or other methods? Let's examine the Scriptures for the answer. Jesus as our example, He went into the water with John the Baptist when He was baptized, *"And Jesus, when he was baptized, went up straight away out of the water"* (Matthew 3:13-16). Another example, the Ethiopian eunuch asked Philip, *"See, here is water; what doth hinder me to be baptized? And he commanded the chariot to stand still: and they both went down into the water, both Philip and the eunuch: and he baptized him"* (Acts 8:36; 8:38). Further, Scripture says *"therefore we are buried with him by baptism into death: that like as Christ was raised from the dead by the glory of the Father, even so, we also should walk in newness of life"* (Romans 6:4). For one to be buried is to be put in the ground, that is, in the grave. Since one is buried with Christ, the baptism water is symbolic to the grave. See Colossians 2:12. The very word baptize signifies or means a burial, to be put under or immersed. The above Scriptures and much more attest to the truth that baptism must be in the name of Jesus, in water, and by immersion.

There is a promise that goes along with the appropriate baptism, *"ye shall receive the gift of the Holy Ghost" (Acts 2:38).* This is the complete new birth that Jesus required when He said, "you must be born again; born of water and spirit" (John 3:3-5). Baptism in itself is not the end, but part of the beginning of our journey with Christ. *"As many of you as have been baptized into Christ have put on Christ"* (Galatians 3:27). It cleanses and makes us a fitting temple for the Spirit of God to dwell there in.

When one has believed the gospel, has repented, is baptized in His name and filled with His Spirit, now you have put on Christ. We do as Christ has done, live as He has lived on earth, think, and speak as He did. We not only have His Spirit but His mind as well, that in all things we might be like Him. To put on Christ, we obligate ourselves to do all His commandments so that we might obtain everlasting life. To be baptized in water in His name without receiving the Holy Ghost still leaves us short of complete salvation. There must be water and spirit to be called one of His (Romans 8:9).

Again, let me ask, how were you baptized? Study these Scriptures carefully, dear friend, if you cannot answer in truth according to the above Scriptures then you should rethink your baptismal experience. **You must be born again**.

PRINCIPLE IV

~5~
LAYING ON OF HANDS

Neglect not the gift that is in thee, which was given thee by prophecy, with the laying on of the hands of the presbytery.

--1 Timothy 4:14

The practice of laying-on of hands appears in both the Old and New Testaments. In the Old Testament there were three general applications:

1) An anointing often used with oil, as a conferring of authority for service. The anointing of priests and kings transpired when they were being prepared to serve. This anointing oil was very special and was not for common use. It was made up of sweet spices (stacte, onycha, galbanum) combined with pure frankincense mixed with pure olive oil. This anointing oil was used to anoint the priest as a preparation for his service in the Tabernacle or temple. No one could duplicate this anointing oil, which was like a perfume, and if they did the penalty was death (Exodus 30:30-38). This holy anointing oil is a type of the Holy Ghost with which God anoints the believer. As with the priesthood, so with Christians today. Until they have been washed and anointed, the individual is not qualified to serve.

2) Identification with the sin sacrifice (Day of Atonement).

> *And Aaron shall lay both his hands upon the head of the live goat, and confess over him all the iniquities of the children of Israel, and all their transgressions in all their sins, putting them **upon the head of the goat**, and shall send him away by the hand of a fit man into the wilderness (Leviticus 16:21).*

3) Laying-on of hands to confer a blessing or favor, and the commission with authority to work in an office. *"And Joshua the son of Nun was full of the spirit of wisdom; for Moses had laid hands upon him: and the children of Israel hearkened unto him, and did as the Lord commanded Moses"* (Deuteronomy 34:9; Numbers 27:18-23).

Old Testament Practices

- Genesis 48:13-20: Jacob blesses Joseph's children.
- Leviticus 9:22: The right hand of blessing (i.e., position of favor).
- Leviticus 16:21: Laying-on hands on the living goat.
- Leviticus 8:14; 8:18; 8:22: Laid hands on the bullock and ram.
- Numbers 27:18-23: Moses laid hands on Joshua.

New Testament References

- Mark 10:13-16: Jesus laid hands on the little children to bless them.
- Luke 24:50: Jesus lifted up His hands to bless.

In the New Testament, there are three applications of laying on of hands instituted by our Lord Jesus and practiced by the apostles beginning with the early days of the church. Since the Scriptures refer to the children of God as kings and priests, then we, like the Old Testament kings and priests, must be anointed as well with the holy anointing oil-the Holy Ghost.

> *But ye are a chosen generation, a royal priesthood, a holy nation, a peculiar people; that ye should shew forth the praises of him who hath called you out of darkness into his marvelous light; which in time past were not a people, but are now the people of God (1 Peter2:9-10).*

> *"And has made us kings and priest unto God and his father; to him be glory and dominion for ever and ever. Amen" (Revelation 1: 6).*

The laying on of hands practice provides a link or channel through which the anointing or virtue of God is passed from one person to the next. The one laying the hands becomes the middle person to the one receiving the blessing. The anointing is not of the person. They have no power of their own. The anointing or virtue comes from God. Virtue comes through a touch. Jesus asked, *"who touched me, virtue has gone out from me"* (Luke 8:43-48).

The three principle uses of laying of hands in the New Testament church beginning on the Day of Pentecost are:

1. In association with receiving the Holy Ghost.
2. Divine healing.
3. Ordination of ministers.

There are more detailed accounts relative to the Holy Ghost and how it is received in the following chapter. There are references in the Book of Acts concerning laying on of hands when individuals receive the Holy Ghost. However, the fact that hands have been laid on an individual does not itself mean they have received the Holy Ghost. The Holy Ghost has the same evidence now as it did on the Day of Pentecost. Many practice laying hands on converts, and by this act alone causes them to believe they have the Spirit of God. This simply is not true. Only

God anoints with His Spirit. *Now he which stablisheth us with you in Christ, and has anointed us, is God"* (2 Corinthians 1:21).

Another very important fundamental of the Pentecostal Apostolic message is that of **divine healing**. This is one of the legacies given to the church. The healings Jesus has done during His ministry were examples of the benefits and privileges members of the Body of Christ are commissioned to do.

And these signs shall follow them that believe; In my name they shall cast out devils; they shall speak with new tongues; and they shall take up serpents; and if they drink any deadly thing, it shall not hurt them; ***they shall lay hands on the sick, and they shall recover*** *(Mark 16:17-18).*

Is any sick among you? Let him call for the elders of the church; and let them pray over him, anointing him with oil in the name of the Lord; and the prayer of faith shall save the sick, and the Lord shall raise him up; and if he hath committed sins, they shall be forgiven (James 5:14-15).

Receiving the Holy Ghost

- Acts 8:14-19: Peter and John laid hands on them to receive the Holy Ghost.
- Acts 19:6: Paul hands laid on him when he received the Holy Ghost.

Anointing Typical of the Holy Ghost

- Exodus 28:41: Anoint Aaron and his sons (Exodus 40:12-15).
- Exodus 30:22-32: The holy anointing oil.
- Leviticus 8:30 The priests were anointed.
- Exodus 29:7: The anointing oil is poured out (profusely to anoint).

- Psalm 45:7: Anointed with the oil of gladness (Hebrews 1:9).
- Psalm 89:20: David is anointed to be king.
- 1 Samuel 16:1: Priests, prophets, and kings were anointed (consecrated) into their office.

Laying On of Hands for Healing
- 2 Kings 5:21: Naaman expected to have hands laid on him.
- Matthew 9:18: Jesus laid hands on the dead daughter of a certain ruler, Jairus.
- Mark 6:5: Jesus laid hands only on a few sick folk.
- Luke 13:11-13: Laid hands on the woman and she was loosed from her infirmity.
- Mark 16:18: These signs follow, lay hands on the sick they will recover.
- Acts 9:12; 9:17: Paul saw one coming to lay hands on him to recover his sight.
- Acts 19:11-12: Special healing by laying on of Paul's hands.
- Acts 5:12: Apostles performed wondrous works.
- Acts 28:9: Paul healed father of Publius.

The third and final practice of laying on of hands in the church is the ordination of the ministry. The ordination service is one of the highlights at the annual Pentecostal Assemblies of the World Conference. It is a time when ministers who have proven themselves worthy by their conduct, academics, and fidelity to the apostles' teaching are commissioned and sent forth to do the work of the ministry and to build up the Kingdom of God as servants of the Most High God.

"Neglect not the gift that is in thee, which is given thee by prophecy, with the laying-on of hands by the presbytery" (1 Timothy 4:14). Here, the gift is the privilege to be a servant of

God and to be commissioned to work in that capacity. The ministry is the greatest and most important work God calls a man to perform. The highest honor a person can receive is to be called into service as a servant for our Lord. From the church at Antioch, the place where they were first called Christians, Saul (Apostle Paul) and Barnabas were sent forth to do the work the Holy Ghost called them to do.

As they ministered to the Lord and fasted, the Holy Ghost said, separate unto me Barnabas and Saul for the work where unto I have called them. And when they had fasted and prayed, and **laid their hands on them**, *they sent them away* (Acts 13:2-3).

Care must be taken, however, not to lay hands suddenly on any person for fear they may not be ready to go and authority is placed on the wrong person (1 Timothy 5:22). The church at Antioch commissioned these two powerful ministers under the auspices of their authority to represent the gospel of Jesus Christ to distant places among the Gentiles.

Laying On of Hands for Ordination (Conferring Authority Commissioned)

- Acts 6:3-6: The seven chosen and commissioned - laid on hands.
- Acts 13:2-3: Barnabus and Paul sent forth by the laying on of hands.
- 1 Timothy 4:14: Timothy had the presbytery lay hands on him.
- 1 Timothy 5:22: We are warned not to lay hands suddenly on any man.
- Acts 19:13-16: Unauthorized laying on of hands.
- John 15:16: Jesus ordained His disciples (Mark 3:14).
- 2 Timothy 1:6: Timothy urged to use his ministry.

- Numbers 8:10-11: Levites offered in service before God.

Jesus Christ is the only one who fulfilled all three principles of Laying On of Hands in the New Testament (Acts 10:38). He is the one who anoints us (2 Corinthians 1:21).

~6~
THE HOLY GHOST: GOD'S PROMISE

The gift of the Holy Spirit is the promise of God unto you.

-- Acts 2:38-39

The goal of every Christian believer is to be saved from the damnation of this life and to inherit the life to come. How to be saved or what it means varies from one church denomination to another. The fact that no two denominations seem to agree in total, causes confusion to those seeking salvation. As a result, people are forced to pick and choose according to their limited knowledge. One church believes in the "three works of grace", another believes there are only two, while a third believes in a one-time experience that lasts for a lifetime. Some believe that once saved they can never be loss. Most Christians trust that by simply believing on the Lord Jesus Christ as their personal Saviour, they are then saved. Another group contends that you are first saved (escape the damnation of Hell) then at some later point they are sanctified-- set apart for God's use. To them, being saved consists of believing on the Lord Jesus Christ followed by some form of water baptism, and at a later time, the Holy Spirit envelops them in a mystical way as an authority for service unto God. However, to the latter this "Holy Spirit" experience is not essential to salvation. This spiritual experience may be associated with speaking in tongues as it is believed by Pentecostal believers whereas others reject the necessity of speaking in other tongues; in either case, they believe the Holy Spirit is an extra blessing God confers on the individual. With these wide range of beliefs it is no wonder many are confused and are willing to 'take the easiest way out', a salvation that takes the least effort on their part. If one is willing to exercise an open mind and accept the Bible's teaching, the confusion will cease and every believer will walk the same path.

The purpose of this writing is to establish what the Bible teaches concerning salvation, particularly the role of the Holy Ghost or Holy Spirit, as the preferred term. The foundation of the church is built on the teachings of *"the apostles and prophets, Jesus Christ himself being the chief corner stone"* (Ephesians 2: 20). Our guide to truth is the apostles' doctrine and not the thoughts and opinions of man. The Scriptures define the Holy Ghost: what it is, who it is, its purpose, what it does, how it is received, and the evidence of its presence. Perhaps one of the most important question the Scriptures will answer is; 'Is the Holy Ghost essential to salvation, and if so, how can one know they have received it?

John the Baptist prophetically articulated that he would baptize with water, but there is one greater than him, that is Jesus Christ, would baptize the people with the Holy Ghost and with fire (Luke 3:16). Some years later, Apostle Paul encountered some believers who were converts of John and asked if they received the Holy Ghost since they had believed. They professed that they had not heard of the Holy Ghost; hence, it was evident they did not have it. Paul asked how they were baptized and proceeded to instruct them about Jesus Christ. When they had received Paul's instruction they were baptized in the name of the Lord Jesus, *"And when Paul had laid his hands upon them, the Holy Ghost came on them; and they spake with tongues and prophesied"* (Acts 19:1-6). This passage of Scripture establishes the fact about the necessity of water baptism in the name of Jesus Christ, and the infilling of the Holy Ghost evidenced by speaking in other tongues.

In the early part of His ministry, Jesus had an encounter with a very intelligent man named Nicodemus and instructed him, *"you must be born again before you can see or enter the Kingdom of God"*. Jesus further explained that this new birth consisted of being born of water (baptized) and of the Spirit (the Holy Ghost). This new birth has two parts: water baptism and receiving the Holy Ghost, where both parts constitute the one new birth experience. Water baptism alone or receiving the Holy Ghost alone is incomplete but the experience must include both if the new birth is to be a complete process (John 3:3-9). When a birth takes place, life begins for that newborn. Similarly, spiritual life begins when one is born from above. In short, one is not saved or spiritually alive until they are fully born again.

Scripture says water baptism is referred to as being buried with Christ, dead to the old way of life, while the Holy Ghost is likened to *"rising again to walk inthe newness of life"* (Romans 6:1-6). This phrase implies a 'spiritual resurrection' enabling one to begin a new life free from sin's guilt. Water baptism is for the remission of sin and is applied to one who has repented by turning from sin and through their faith in the shed blood of Christ, and is cleared of the charges of guilt. They are dead to sin and ready to receive the "Spirit of Life" (Acts 2:38). The Holy Ghost will make Himself known to the believer because he will speak with other tongues as the spirit gives utterance (Acts 2:2-4; 14:18; Isaiah 28:11; Acts 10:45-46; Acts 19:6).

The last words of Jesus to His apostles, they were to return to Jerusalem and *"wait for the promise of the Father which ye have heard from me"* (Acts 1:4). The apostles could not move forward until the promise had been fulfilled in them. The promise was the Holy Ghost. Many will argue that the disciples received the Holy Ghost soons after the resurrection of Jesus and before His final ascension. They point to John 20:22, where Jesus breathed on them and said receive ye the Holy Ghost. This was not a 'present time experience' but a promise that would be fulfilled not many days from the Day of Pentecost (Acts 1:5). The Day of Pentecost transpired ten days following the ascension of Jesus into Heaven (Acts 2:1-4). The scriptural reference John 7:37-39, is further proof where Jesus speaks of living water flowing out of the belly and is identified with the Spirit, which He said they should receive, because the *"Holy Ghost was not yet given because Jesus was not yet glorified"* (v. 39). Notice, this scriptural reference used the term spirit synonymous with Holy Ghost.

Jesus speaks of the Holy Ghost as *"the promise of the Father"* (Acts 1:4; Luke 24:49). On the Day of Pentecost, Peter quotes the Prophet Joel (Joel 2:28-32), *"That in the last days, saith God, I will pour out of my Spirit upon all flesh"* (Acts 2:16-17). Moreover, Ezekiel prophesies *"and I will put my Spirit within you and cause you to walk in my statutes, and ye shall keep my judgments, and do them"* (Ezekiel 36:25-27). Isaiah utters the words, *"I will pour my Spirit upon all thy seed, and my blessing upon thine offspring"* (Isaiah 44:3). Also, see Zechariah 12:10. These Old Testament promises were to Israel as a nation, but they rejected their Messiah, Jesus Christ, and as a nation forfeited their claim to these promises (Luke 19:41-44; Matthew 23:37-39). The promise of the Holy Ghost was denied to the nation of Israel and was given to those individuals who believed in Jesus: first the Jews and later the Gentiles (Acts 8 and Acts 10).

There is one thing of special note in those prophetic promises. God said He would pour out His spirit upon all flesh. The Holy Ghost poured out on the Day of Pentecost was God's own Spirit, and God would do the pouring (2 Corinthians 1:21-22). As we will see later, this Holy Ghost is also the Spirit of Christ (John 14:16-18). Are there two Spirits? No! There is but one spirit which is God's Spirit. The Spirit of Christ and the Holy Ghost are one and the same thing, *"For by one spirit are we all baptized into one body"* (1 Corinthians 12:13).

How then can we define the Holy Ghost? It is the Spirit of Christ that comes to dwell in us. It empowers us with the ability to subdue our spirit to fulfill the will and desire of God's spirit. On the Day of Pentecost, the Holy Ghost was poured out in a rather unexpected manner. If those 120 individuals in the upper room had been fully acquainted with the Scriptures, they may not have been so mystified by the arrival of the Holy Ghost (Acts 2:1-4). Speaking in tongues was God's method. Why did He choose tongues? Perhaps it was because the tongue is the most unruly member of our body and with His spirit, He captures control of our being. God used tongues to divide mankind at the Tower of Babel (Genesis 2:6-9), and then used the same method to join believers into a single body by giving them the language to speak. The Prophet Isaiah shared the method centuries before it happened. *"For with stammering lips and another tongue will He speak to his people. To whom he said, this is the rest wherewith ye may cause the weary to rest"* (Isaiah 28:11-12). Tongues are God's doing. Many in the latter-day Pentecostal communities are using all manners of tactics to give the Holy Ghost, all of which are in error. The only valid way to receive the Holy Spirit is by God's initiative. He and only He gives His Spirit when the heart of man is ready to receive Him. Teaching one to speak some phrases, breathing on the candidate seeking the Holy Spirit, just believing it's there, or laying on of hands per-se are not God's methods. When one receives the Holy Ghost, it is because God fills them with His Spirit and they will speak with other tongues *"as the spirit of God gives them utterance"* (Acts 2:4). It is an act of God and not man.

Much rhetoric is made about speaking in tongues. The power of God is not in the tongues spoken, but it's in His Spirit that comes to dwell in the person. Tongues are a sign, a very important sign to be sure, but the power of the Holy Ghost is Christ in us. The initial evidence of the presence of the Holy Ghost at the new birth is speaking in other tongues. This is verified in the Book of Acts during each instance the Holy Ghost was received by a person or a group of people. The real proof of the Holy Ghost beyond the initial evidence is the lifestyle in the days following the birth. When a baby is born the cry is the first sign of life, after that, activity determines the life present. Do not confuse the "gift of tongues" with receiving the Holy Ghost. Though they may sound alike, there is a difference. Speaking in other tongues when receiving the Holy Ghost is God's business on how He decided to administer the gift of the Holy Spirit, however, the gift of tongues is one of the several gifts that God gives and can be used at will by the possessor of that gift.

Difference Between the Evidence and the Gift of Tongues

In the *Greek-English Lexicon,* the gift of the Holy Spirit as found in the Book of Acts, is the *dynamis* or dynamic power of the Most High God (Acts 1:7). The gift of the Holy Ghost is made evident when the recipient initially speaks in an unknown tongue whereas the gift of diverse tongues is one of the nine gifts distributed by Holy Spirit to the believer. It may appear confusing but when you rightly divide the Scriptures it becomes very discernible. According to the Scriptures, on the Day of Pentecost, the believers were all filled with the Holy Ghost and began to speak with other tongues as the Spirit gave them utterance. On Pentecost and since, everyone who has received the baptism of the Holy Ghost has spoken in tongues.

The Book of Acts records the acceptance of the gift (singular) of the Holy Ghost, whereas the twelfth chapter of 1 Corinthians deals with the operation of the gifts (plural) of the Holy Ghost. According to the *Greek-English Lexicon* of the New Testament, the term "gift" as in the gift of the Holy Ghost means *dorea* or *doron*, which is the sacrificial life of Christ (Acts 2:38). The term "gifts" as in diversities of gifts (1 Corinthians 12) is derived from the term *chrisma*, which means religious qualification or mariculous faculty. One cannot qualify for the diversities of gifts until they are the recipient of the gift, initial evidence of the Holy Spirit speaking in tongues.

On the Day of Pentecost, Peter provided the formula for salvation. Scripture says, *"Then Peter said unto them, Repent, and be baptized every one of you in the name of Jesus Christ for the remission of sins, and ye shall receive the gift of the Holy Ghost"* (Acts 2:38). This is not in conflict with the great commission Jesus gave to his disciples in Matthew 28:19. In fact, it is the implementation of the commission to preach and baptize. The instruction to the disciples was the use of the **name** (not names) of the Father, of the Son, and of the Holy Ghost. Each of the above are titles of the **one name** to be used. If we knew, the name of the Father, Son, and Holy Ghost there would be no problem in using the proper name. The **name is** Jesus. Peter knew this and gave an instruction that followed repentance, baptism in the name of Jesus Christ was the next step. Water baptism does not end the process. Next, Peter says the candidate of salvation was to *receive the gift of the Holy Ghost*. Notice the word receive, this wonderful gift is the responsibility of the candidate to open their heart and permit Christ to enter. God gives His Spirit, but we must be prepared to receive it. The next word is 'gift', which is something given by the giver. It is not earned or begged for. It is given purely as a gift and only God gives this precious gift to the repentant and believing individual. Too many individuals spend too much time working to obtain something that God has promised to be freely received as a gift. Peter declared this gift was, *"for you (Jews), your children and all who were afar off"*. God had to convince Peter in a most dramatic fashion who the 'afar off' were in Acts chapter 10.

Since the Book of Acts is a historical account of the beginning and progress of the church, we can observe how and what role the Holy Ghost played in this growing church. Is there a common thread of action? The second chapter of the Book of Acts described the first occurrence of the Holy Ghost filling individuals. It was accompanied by *speaking in "other tongues as the Spirit gave them utterance"* (Acts 2:4). Following the upper room experience of the Holy Ghost filling the One Hundred and Twenty gathered together, many other believers were added to the church during those early days. There is no reason to believe these newly added believers did not experience the same thing as the one hundred and twenty on the Day of Pentecost (Acts 1:14-16). The next occurrence of receiving the Holy Ghost is in Acts chapter 8, Philip went to the City of Samaria where a large group of people gave heed to Philip's ministry. The message was the Kingdom of God (new birth) and the name of Jesus. They believed Philip's message and were baptized in the name of the Lord Jesus (Acts 8:12-16). The one thing missing was the Holy Ghost. Peter and John were summoned and when they arrived in Samaria, they laid hands on these newly baptized converts and they received the Holy Ghost (v. 16). Something visible happened as seen in verse 18. What they received was the "Gift of God" (v. 20). The people of Samaria were neither Jews nor Gentiles and represented the beginning of the expansion of the church to non-Jewish communities.

The next move of the Holy Ghost was to the Gentiles community. Cornelius with his household was chosen and Peter had an extraordinary vision from God, a vision he later understood to mean that the Gentiles would be privileged to receive this marvelous gift of the Holy Ghost. While Peter was preaching to Cornelius and his company, something wonderful happened, the Holy Ghost fell on Cornelius and those who "heard the Word". They began to speak in tongues and magnify God. In order to fulfill the new birth requirements, Peter commanded them to be baptized in the name of the Lord, which is Jesus Christ. When Peter returned to Jerusalem, he shared with his fellow disciples about the conversion of Cornelius and his household. He informed then that the Gentiles had received the Holy Ghost the same way we did in the beginning. The rest of the apostles then remembered John the Baptist's words *"Ye shall be baptized with the Holy Ghost"* and were convinced that *"God also to the Gentiles granted repentance unto life"* (Acts 11:15-17).

If you will notice that with Philip at Samaria, they were baptized in the Name of Jesus, but when Peter and John came laying hands on them, these baptized believers received the Holy Ghost thus completing both parts of the new birth, water and Spirit. The new birth process was not realized until both parts were completed. Cornelius and his house received the Holy Ghost, speaking in other tongues and were entirely commanded to be baptized in the **name of the Lord, Jesus**. As with those in Samaria, the new birth of Cornelius was incomplete until water and Sprit had been accomplished. This is further proof that one has not completed the new birth experience process until they are baptized in the name of Jesus and filled with the Holy Ghost evidenced by speaking in other tongues. One without the other is simply not enough. It must be noted that receiving the Holy Ghost is not always accompanied by the laying on of hands. In the case of Cornelius, laying on of hands was not mentioned at all. The last description of receiving the Holy Ghost is found in Acts 19:1-6. Paul, finding certain disciples, asked if they had received the Holy Ghost since they had believed.

The Holy Ghost is not some add-on experience, or some optional experience. It is the main event for believers. There were certain believers at Ephesus that professed they did not know about the Holy Ghost then Apostle Paul asked, *how were you baptized?* They responded and said, it was John's baptism. Paul answered them, John's baptism was unto repentance but pointed to one greater than him, Christ Jesus. When they heard this, without any argument, they were baptized in the name of the Lord (Acts 11:15-17). Paul laid hands on them and they received the Holy Ghost, speaking in tongues and prophesied (vs. 5-6). Once again we see the combination of water baptism in the name of Jesus and being filled with the Holy Ghost, speaking in tongues to complete the new birth. This experience proves if one is baptized contrary to Scripture they must be rebaptized before they can be "saved".

The historical records in the Book of Acts relating to receiving the Holy Ghost and the command of Jesus about being born again, are proof of the necessity of having the Holy Ghost. There is, however, one more powerful Scripture that expresses the absolute necessity of having the Holy Ghost. To be truly saved, one must become the possession of Christ.

Besides being the Spirit of Christ, what is the Holy Ghost and what does it do?

1.   The Holy Ghost is eternal life. There is no hope of eternal life without it. *"And this is the record, that God has given to us eternal life, and this life is in his Son. He that hath the Son hath life; and he that hath not the Son of God hath not life"* (1 John

5:11-12). What does it mean to have the Son of God? It means to have His Spirit, the Holy Ghost (Romans 8:9; John 1:4; John 17:2-3; Galatians 3:27-29; John 4:4). The Holy Ghost is the quickening power of God that resurrects us from the deadness of sin and trespasses (Ephesians 2:1-4).

2. The Holy Ghost is God's seal on the believer that they are God's possession purchased with His shed blood. By having the seal of the Holy Ghost, a testimony is presented to the world that my soul belongs to God (Ephesians 1:13; 2 Corinthians 1:21-22). It is also the earnest (proof) of our inheritance or Christ's assurance we have an inheritance reserved in Heaven for us (Ephesians 1:14; 1 Peter 1:4-5).

3. The Holy Ghost is God's power in us. Scriptures says, *"Ye shall receive power, after that the Holy Ghost is come upon you: and ye shall be witnesses unto me both in Jerusalem, and in all Judaea, and in Samaria, and unto the uttermost part of the earth"* (Acts 1:8). The *Koine Greek* word for power is dunamis, which the *Analytical Lexicon of the Greek New Testament* defines with reference to Acts 1:8 as, able to produce a strong effect power, might, strength and as supernatural manifestations of power miracle, wonder, powerful deed. The word *dunamis* is used ten times in the Book of Acts and is always in reference to God's power, miracles, signs, and wonders. When the Bible uses the word dunamis, it never refers to human strength or ability but to God's power through mankind. It is His power alone that guards the believer, while it forms our character as we walk in His power and glorify Him.

It is the dunamis to fight Satan and to overcome self-will and the world. With this power comes the authority to preach and to witness in His name. No one is ready to face Satan, live for God, or minister in His Kingdom until they have been endued with the power of the Holy Ghost. Many are preaching, working miracles, casting out demons to no avail, simply because God does not know them. Why does God not know them? Because they are ministering without His authority and without possessing His Spirit, the Holy Ghost. They are not on God's payroll and are at the Day of Judgment, commanded to depart because "*I never knew you*" (Matthew 7:21-23).

4. Having the Holy Ghost is to be made a partaker of His divine nature (2 Peter 1:4). To be in Christ, one becomes a new creature. Scripture says, old things are passed away and all things have become new (2 Corinthians 5:17). As a new creature, one can live in a manner that is pleasing to God and free to exercise the divine attributes of God.

5. Jesus described the Holy Ghost as another comforter (John 14:16), the paraclete to stand with us and plead our case. This comforter is identified as the Holy Ghost in verse 26. It is the "Spirit of Truth" (v. 17) which was in Jesus and would in the future abide in the believers. The Holy Ghost could not come until the body of Jesus had departed earth. When Jesus returns, it would be in spirit form as the abiding presence in each believer. *"It is expedient for you that I go away: for if I go not away, the comforter will not come unto you. But if I depart I will send him unto you"* (John 16:7; John 14:18-20).

6. The function of the Holy Ghost is to guide us into all truth and to reveal things to come (John 16:13). It is a teacher and a memory shaker (John 14:26), and it is a keeper, a preserver unto the day of His appearing.

7. Lastly, the Holy Spirit is the anointing God gives to those who will accept the terms of the new birth and embrace His name in baptism and receive the gift so freely given to the honest believer of the gospel. The anointing is God's personal touch that empowers one to work for Him and do His will.

Who can receive the Holy Ghost? Anyone who believes in the Lord Jesus Christ and the work He accomplished on the cross and in Heaven. Those who are willing to obey His commands and walk in His footsteps. All that is needed is to repent and be baptized in the name of Jesus Christ and be ready to receive His gift. The Spirit is given to those that ask (Luke 11:13). Many do not know about the wonderful gift of God and are much like the woman Jesus met at the well. The gift of God is living water, a well of water where one can drink and refresh their soul (John

4:10-14; Isaiah 12:13; Isaiah 28:11-12). Further, Jesus identifies the Holy Ghost as *"rivers of living water flowing out from the belly"* (John 7:37-39; Psalm 46:4).

Hopefully, you, the reader will prayerfully study the Scriptures outlined in this chapter and come to know for yourselves the saving power of Jesus Christ, our Lord. May the grace and peace of God be with you, now and forever.

PRINCIPLE V

~7~
RESURRECTION OF THE DEAD

If there be no resurrection of the dead, then is Christ not risen.

-- 1 Corinthians 15:13

Resurrection is the act of being raised from the dead; to cause to stand up from the dead, to live again, or to die no more (Romans 6:1-9). The book, *The Seven Stages of the Resurrection,* outlines the doctrine of the resurrection of the dead as having two distinct parts separated by 1,000 years. The 'first resurrection' (Revelation 20:5-6) has seven sections or seven distinct times of occurrences beginning with the resurrection of Jesus, then the rapture of the church, and the last section will transpire in the midpoint of the tribulation. Rapture is the catching away of the church, referring to those alive at the appearing of the Lord Jesus Christ. Those in the first resurrection are called "blessed and holy". The second or last resurrection occurs at the white throne of judgment when the rest of the dead, both good and bad, will be resurrected to stand before God's throne to be judged out of the "books" (Revelation 20:12). Those in the

"Book of Life" will be granted eternal life and all others are consigned to the "Lake of Fire" which is eternal damnation. Between the first and second resurrections, there is 1,000 years of peace where Christ will sit on the throne of David and reigns as king over all the earth (Zechariah 14:9). This Kingdom Age era is referred to as the Millennial Kingdom. Following the Kingdom Age, Satan will be loosed from his prison for a short time to gather the Gentiles into his camp. The final punishment of God is exercised against the earth with fire out of Heaven to devour those deceived by the Devil (2 Peter 3:10-13; Revelation 19:7-11). The next scene is the 'white throne of judgment' preceded by the second resurrection where all the dead are raised to be judged according to the deeds done in the body. Those of the first resurrection will not be part of this final judgment (Revelations 20:1-8).

The Seven Sections of the First Resurrection

1. Jesus Christ, the first fruits (1 Corinthians 15:20; 15:23; Philippians 3:20-21).
2. The Old Testament believers following the resurrection of Jesus (Matthew 27:52-53; 1 Corinthians 15:23).
3. The resurrection and rapture of the saints (1 Thessalonians 4:13-17; Revelation 4:1; 1 Corinthians 15: 51-52).

The tribulation begins at this point and the remaining four sections occur during the first three and a half years of the tribulation.

4. The Palm Bearers (Revelation 7:9-11; Revelation 6:9-11).
5. The 144,000 sealed of Israel.
6. The two witnesses, Moses and Elijah at the close of the three and a half years ministry to Israel (Zechariah 4:11-14; Revelation 11:3-12; Malachi 4:4-6).
7. Those beheaded for the witness of Jesus Christ (Revelation 20: 4).

Everyone in his own order (1 Corinthians 15:20-23; Daniel 12:13).

The doctrine of the Resurrection of the Dead is one of the most fundamental of all Apostolic message. Paul defended the resurrection of Christ as explained in these terms:

> *But if there be no resurrection of the dead, then is Christ not risen. And if Christ is not risen, then is our preaching vain and your faith is also vain. Yea, and we are found false witnesses of God - And if Christ be not raised, your faith is vain; ye are yet in your sins. Then they also which are fallen asleep in Christ are perished (1 Corinthians 15:13-18).*

> *Concerning his Son Jesus Christ our Lord, which was made of the seed of David according to the flesh; and declared to be the Son of God, according to the spirit of holiness, by the resurrection from the dead (Romans 1:3-4).*

It is abundantly apparent by these Scriptures that deliverance from sin and the hope of eternal life is totally dependent on the facts of the resurrection of Jesus Christ. But thank God, Jesus came forth from the grave as appointed and our hope is valid and intact. Before His death Jesus promised, *"because I live, you shall live also"* (John 14:19). The doctrine of the resurrection did not begin with the New Testament, but was a hope found in the Old Testament and made a reality by the resurrection of Jesus Christ. The biblical character Job, asked a rhetorical question, *"if a man die, shall he live again? All the days of my appointed time will wait until my change comes"* (Job 14:14). And again Job exclaims, *"for I know that my redeemer liveth, and he shall stand at the latter day upon the earth: and though after my skin worms destroy this body, yet in my flesh I shall see God: whom I shall see for myself"* (Job 19:25-27).

Abraham believed God and even though the promises were not fulfilled in his lifetime, but by faith he was assured they would be in the future.

> *These all died in faith, not having received the promises, but having seen them afar off, and were persuaded of them, embraced them, and confessed that they were strangers and pilgrims on the earth -- but now they desire a better country, that is, an heavenly: wherefore God is not ashamed to be called their God; for he hath prepared for them a city (Hebrews 11:13-16).*

Abraham knew that the promise of God hinged on the 'seed' that would come from his loin, Isaac. When God tested Abraham and told him to offer his son Isaac on the altar, Abraham did not flinch but was set to carry out the command of his God. The fact that Isaac would die was not disturbing to Abraham, for he knew *"that God was able to raise him up, even from the dead; from whence also he received him in a figure"* (Hebrews 11:19; Genesis 22:1-14). He proceeded to offer up his son. It was not Isaac who provided hope for life after death but the true seed, Jesus Christ (Galatians 3:16).

David expressed his hope in the resurrection by linking his hope of the resurrection to the Messiah (Psalm 16:8-10),

> *I have set the Lord always before me: because he is at my right hand, I shall not be moved, therefore my heart is glad, and my soul rejoiceth: my flesh shall also rest in hope. For thou wilt not leave my soul in hell [the grave] neither wilt thou suffer thine Holy One to see corruption.*

Daniel is assured by Michael, the archangel:

> *And many of them that sleep in the dust of the earth shall awake, some to everlasting life, and some to shame and everlasting contempt"* and "*But go thou thy way till the end be: for thou shalt rest [sleep in the grave] and stand [be*

raised to life again] in thy lot at the end of the days (Daniel 12:2; 12:13).

All of the prophets one way or another confirmed the hope of being raised to life again and support the reality of a resurrection. The fact of a final and eternal judgment is also proof that the soul that dies will be raised from the grave, to be judged of deeds while they were alive.

Life after death could not be hoped for until the cause of death had been conquered. Sin brought its terrible sentence, 'the soul that sins, it shall surely die'; this would remain in force until the sting of death could be removed. It was Jesus who died and fought the forces of Hell and came out of the grave victorious, holding in His hand the keys to death, Hell, and the grave. *"I am he that liveth, and was dead; and, behold, I am alive for evermore, Amen; and have the keys of Hell [grave] and of death"* (Revelation 1:18). With the resurrection of Jesus, death no longer had the power to hold forever. *"Now if we be dead with Christ, we believe that we shall also live with him: knowing that christ being raised from the dead dieth no more; death hath no more dominion over him"* (Romans 6:8-9). Since Christ liveth forevermore, and we shall live with Him, then those who have the Spirit of Christ in them also will be raised to die no more. Once again, the resurrection of Jesus Christ is the key to man's hope of being resurrected.

It is certainly a false hope on the part of anyone to believe that death ends it all and this life is all one can expect. Suicide victims will be greatly surprised on the Day of Judgment to realize the solution to their problems only made it eternally worse for them. Still, others believe that once in the torment of hell fire, they will eventually be annihilated, totally burned up and cease to exist. If Hell is that short, then Heaven must have an end as well. It is a relief, indeed, to know from the Scriptures that neither of these beliefs are true.

There is a difference between being raised from the dead and being resurrected from the dead. There are several accounts in the Scriptures where individuals were raised from the dead.

Examples, Elijah raised to life a woman's son who had died (1 Kings 17:17-23), Elisha raised the Shunammite's son back to life (2 Kings 4:32-37), Jesus raised the daughter of Jarius (Luke 8:49-56), the widow's son (Luke 7:11-15), Lazarus (John 11:43-44), Peter raised Dorcas (Acts 9:40), Paul raised the young man who fell out of the window and died (Acts 20:9-10). Since they are not with us today, it is obvious they must have died and returned to the grave to await their resurrection.

Jesus, who raised Lazarus from his tomb of four days, comforts Mary and Martha, Lazarus's sisters, with these words: *"Thy brother shall live again"* (John 11:23-26). The people in the days of Jesus believed there was resurrection, Martha answered, *"I know he shall rise again in the resurrection at the last day"*. In short Jesus says Martha, I know that, but to prove the resurrection power is mine I will bring him forth from the grave, now. Then adds these precious words: "I am the resurrection and the life: he that believeth in me, though he were dead, yet shall he live: And whosoever liveth in me shall never die. Believeth thou this?" (John 11:23-26). Not only does Jesus declare that He has the power to raise from the dead, He is life, eternal life, and will give that life to those who will believe in Him according to the Scriptures. Note the following Scriptures: 1 John 5:11-12; 5:21-29; John 17:2-3. Each of these Scriptures declares that to have Jesus Christ is to have eternal life.

There was a religious group called the Sadducees, who did not believe in a resurrection, in angels, or anything supernatural. These Sadducees presented a parable to Jesus concerning a marriage relationship in the 'hereafter'. Their perspective of the resurrection was in error and Jesus answers them in this manner,

> *But as touching the resurrection of the dead, have you not read that which was spoken unto you by God, saying, I am the God of Abraham, and the God of Isaac, and the God of Jacob? God is not the God of the dead, but of the living"* (Matthew 22:23-32).

It might be said, there is a spiritual resurrection for those who are saved. Paul uses baptism as a metaphor:

Know ye not, that so many of us as were baptized into Jesus Christ, were baptized into his death? Therefore we are buried with him by baptism into death: that like as Christ was raised up from the dead by the glory of the Father, even so we also should walk in newness of life (Romans 6:3-4).

When the cause of death has been removed from the soul by the blood of Christ and the soul stands justified before God, the death sentence has been removed and it now lives. The soul has been delivered from death and quickened by the Spirit of God to live for Him. *"I am crucified with Christ: nevertheless I live; yet not I, but Christ liveth in me: and the life which I now live in the flesh I live by the faith of the Son of God, who loved me and gave his life for me"* (Galatians 2:20). This life in Christ is, in one sense, a spiritually resurrected life, a new life that is now free from the deadness of sin and made alive before God. *"Likewise reckon ye also yourselves to be dead indeed unto sin, but alive unto God through Jesus Christ our Lord"* (Romans 6:11). The body will return to dust, but the soul that is filled with the Spirit of Life, lives on and the 'second death', eternal judgment, cannot touch it anymore. Notice, the body is not to be saved and neither will this body be resurrected. It is the soul which will be resurrected and given a new body from God out of Heaven (2 Corinthians 5:1-3).

The church has a part in the first resurrection, which will occur just prior to the beginning of the tribulation period consisting of seven years. Our comfort and hope is found in 1 Thessalonians 4:13-18,

For this we say unto you by the word of the Lord, that we which are alive and remain unto the coming of the Lord shall not prevent them which are asleep. For the Lord himself will descend from heaven with a shout, with the voice of the archangel, and with the trump of God, and the

dead in Christ shall rise first: then we which are alive and remain shall be caught up together with them in the clouds, to meet the lord in the air: and so shall we ever be with the Lord.

The appearing of Jesus is not to be confused with His second coming. The appearing is just prior to the tribulation period, while His second coming is at the end of the tribulation and is the beginning of the millennium. The rapture of the New Testament church will be at His appearing (Hebrews 9:28), and will appear the second time without sin unto salvation. As Jesus departed from the Mount of Olives, His second return will be at the same point (Acts 1:11-12; Revelation 1:7).

The appearance will be quick "*in a twinkling of an eye, at the last trump: for the trumpet shall sound, and the dead shall be raised incorruptible, and we shall be changed*" (1 Corinthians 15:52). In biblical times, there were only two terms that described quickness. The twinkling of the eye and the flash of lightning from the east to the west. Today, science has divided the second into milliseconds and nanoseconds which are shorter measurements of time. The return of Jesus is referred to as one coming as a thief in the night because the date and time will not be announced. These two phrases describe the suddenness and unexpectedness of the rapture (1 Thessalonians 5:2).

Scriptural References of the Resurrection Doctrine

- Job 14:14-15: I will wait until my change comes.
- Job 19:25-27: After the skin worms eat my flesh, in my flesh will I see God.
- Hebrews 11:17-19: Abraham's faith in receiving Isaac from the dead.
- Isaiah 26:19: The earth shall cast out her dead.
- Psalm 17:15: I will be satisfied when I awake in His likeness.

- Psalm 16:9-10: My soul will not be left in Hell; the grave.
- Acts 2:24-31: Not leave my soul in Hell or thy Holy One to see corruption.
- Psalms 49:15: God to redeem the soul from the power of the grave.
- Isaiah 25:8: He will swallow up death in victory.
- Hosea 13:14: Ransomed from the power of the grave; death.
- 1 Samuel 2:6: The Lord will kill and make alive, brings up from the grave.
- Daniel 12:2-3: Many sleep in dust will rise up.
- Daniel 12:13: Daniel to stand in his lot at the end of days.
- Ezekiel 37:4: Can these dry bones live?
- Isaiah 26:20-21: The resurrection and rapture of the church (hide thyself a little moment).
- Isaiah 26:19: Israel's hope to rise from the dead.
- Revelation 20:5-6: Blessed and Holy are those in the first resurrection.
- Acts 4:2: Resurrection from the dead preached through Jesus.
- John 11:24-26: Jesus, the resurrection and the life.
- Romans 1:4: Jesus declared to be the Son of God by the resurrection from the dead.
- 1 Corinthians 15:4: He rose according to the Scriptures.
- Acts 1:3: The resurrection of Jesus confirmed by many infallable proofs.
- 1 Corinthians 15:12-21: The resurrection the corner stone of our salvation.

- Acts 23:6: Paul's hope of the resurrection.
- Acts 24:15: There is a resurrection of the just and unjust.
- John 5:24-29: The resurrection unto life and unto death (judgment).
- 1 Timothy 1:10: The hope of the resurrection brought to us through the gospel.
- 1 Peter 1:3: An inheritance assured by the resurrection of Jesus.
- Hebrews 11:35: Through faith they look to receive a better resurrection.
- Hebrews 11:13-16: These all died in faith having seen a better place afar off.
- Acts 26:6-8: Why is it thought incredible for God to raise the dead?
- Romans 8:11: The Spirit of God to quicken our mortal bodies.
- Romans 8:20-25: The resurrection our hope.
- 1 Corinthians 15:42-54: Our change in the resurrection.
- 2 Corinthians 5:1-4: Put on our new house not made with hands.
- 1 Thessalonians 5:10: Whether we wake or sleep, live with Him.
- Romans 8:8-9: He died and rose to become Lord of the dead and living.
- Luke 14:14: Shall be recompensed at the resurrection of the just.
- Mark 12:24-26: In the resurrection we will be like the angels, we will not marry. God is the God of the living and not the dead.

- Matthew 22:30-32: God is God of the living and not the dead.
- John 14:19: Because I live you shall live also.
- Revelation 20:4-6: The first resurrection.
- Revelation 20:12: The second resurrection.
- Matthew 25:31-46: Resurrection unto life and death (John 5:28-29).
- Hebrews 11:17-19: Abraham believed in the resurrection.
- Matthew 19:28: In the regeneration.
- Luke 20:35-37: Jesus assures the fact of the resurrection.

As can be seen by this list of Scriptures, the Old Testament speaks of the resurrection as hope, but the New Testament the validity of that hope because of the resurrection of Jesus Christ. Without the resurrection, we have nothing to stand on. It is the hope of the resurrection that enables us to endure the hardships of life in attempt to gain a better life in the end; eternal life with Christ (Romans 4:25; 5:10; 8: 34; 1 Peter 3:21).

The righteous or blessed are those who have part in the first resurrection implies a good moral conduct. Only God is the judge of righteousness. The holy ones are those anointed with the Holy Ghost and consecrated before God. Jesus gives some evidence that the Old Testament patriarchs: Abraham, Isaac, Jacob, and all the prophets will be in the kingdom of God:

> *There shall be weeping and gnashing of teeth, when ye shall see Abraham, and Isaac, and Jacob, and all the Prophets, in the kingdom of God and you yourselves cast out. And they shall come from the east, and from the west, and from the north and from the south, and shall sit down in the kingdom of God (Luke 13:28-29).*

- Matthew 24:7: As lightning flashes from east to west so is the coming of Christ.
- 1 Thessalonians 5:1-4 Coming as a thief in the night.
- Revelation 16:15: He will come as a thief; keep thy garments prepared.
- Matthew 24:42-44: Watch, you know not the hour of His coming (Luke 12:39-40).
- Hebrews 9:28: He appears the second time without sin unto salvation.
- 2 Timothy 4:1; 4:8: Judged at His appearing.
- Titus 2:13: Looking for the glorious appearing of Jesus Christ.
- Colossians 3:4: When Christ who is our life shall appear.

The "companions of the bride" (Psalm 45:11; 45:14), and the bride's attendants (Revelation 7:14). These are those that will be part of the resurrection that takes place during the first half of the tribulation. The palm bearers along with those who will be beheaded for their faith in Christ because they refused to take the mark of the beast.

At the appearing of Christ only the raptured or resurrected individuals that have experienced the new birth-the New Testament church will see Him. The Scriptures say every eye shall behold Him at His second coming (Revelation 1:7).

There are two branches of the second resurrection:

A. The resurrection of the just (righteous) unto life.
B. The resurrection of the wicked unto everlasting damnation. This is the second death.

- Matthew 25:31-46: The sheep and goats (righteous and wicked) are judged.
- John 5:28-29: The resurrection unto life and unto damnation.

- Luke 14:14: The resurrection of the just.
- Acts 24:15: The resurrection of the just and the unjust.
- Revelation 20:11-15: All the dead, both small and great will be judged.
- Psalm 9:7-8; 9:17: The wicked will be turned into Hell.

Our Physical Appearance in the Resurrection

Little is said in the Bible concerning how we shall appear in the resurrection. The few Scriptures that provide some understanding are listed below.

- 1 John 3:1-3: It does not yet appear what we shall be, but we shall be like Him.
- Philippians 3:20-21: We shall be fashioned like unto His glorious body.
- Luke 20:33-37: There will be no marriages in Heaven.
- Revelation 20:6: We will never die again, but have eternal life.
- Corinthians 15:49: We will bear the image of the heavenly.
- Corinthians 15:35-44: Our change, what we will be like.
- Corinthians 5:1-4: We have a new house from Heaven.

PRINCIPLE VI

~8~
ETERNAL JUDGMENT

Every idle word men may speak, they will give account of it in the day of judgment.

-- Matthew 12:36

God has judged the earth numerous times since the existence of man. The first judgment was against Adam and Eve, when they were cast out of the Garden of Eden. After about 1656 years, God was grieved with the wickedness of man on the earth and resented that he made man (Genesis 4-8). But Noah found grace in the eyes of God and was commanded to build an ark providing an escape from the impending judgment that was to come. Noah became the means of saving the world at that time, but no one believed his message and only eight individuals (souls) were spared (saved) from the flood that destroyed the entire human race and every living thing that drew the breath of life (Genesis 6 and 7; 1 Peter 3:20).

The next major judgment came in the lifetime of Abraham, who pleaded for the rescue of his nephew, Lot and his family. The cities of Sodom, Gomorra, Admah, and Zeboim were destroyed because of the filthy and ungodly lifestyle practiced by the inhabitants. Lot, his wife, and two daughters were spared from the mass destruction (Genesis 18 and 19). Also, Israel as a nation was judged many times for their misconduct. In each case, God provided a means whereby the judgment could be avoided. The person, people, or nation who would repent and accept God's terms of deliverance will not be judged. Will the righteous God judge the wicked and the righteous alike? No!

There is yet one more major judgment to face this world. The term for this is the Time of Tribulation. This worldwide judgment will last for seven years and will be divided by two. The second half is referred to as the Great Tribulation where God will be at war with man and the destruction will be so severe during those seven years that only one-sixth of the human population will survive (Ezekiel 39:2). The period is also referred to as the following: Jacob's Trouble (Jeremiah 30:4-7); The Day of the Lord (Isaiah 13:9; Joel 2:1); The Day of His Wrath or Indignation (Zephaniah 1:15; Isaiah 26:20); The Great and Terrible Day of the Lord (Joel 2:31; Malachi 4:5); The Great Tribulation (Matthew 24:21). The last event as documented by all the prophets including, Isaiah, Ezekiel, and Daniel is detailed in the Book of Matthew (24).

Before the tribulation begins, the one event the living church is looking for is the rapture of the church. *"Come my people, enter thou into thy chambers, and shut thy doors about thee: hide thyself for a little moment, until my indignation be over past"* (Isaiah 26:20).

> *If we believe that Jesus died and rose again, even so them also which sleep in Jesus will God bring with him. For the Lord himself shall descend from heaven with a shout, with the voice of the archangel and with the trump of God: and the dead in Christ shall rise first Then we which are alive shall be caught up together with them in the clouds, to meet the Lord in the air, and so shall we ever be with the Lord (1 Thessalonians 4:14-18).*

This horrible time on earth will end with the Battle of Armageddon (Revelation 16:16). When the great battle between God and man, led by the Anti-Christ concludes then the second coming of Jesus Christ will take place. He will establish a kingdom called the Millennial Kingdom, where Christ will sit on the throne of David and rule the world for a 1,000 years. The raptured church will reign with Him as kings and priests unto God. *"And hath made us unto our God kings and priests: and we shall reign on earth"* (Revelation 5:10). None of the above judgments found in the Old Testament will involve the soul of man. The body in death is the part of man that suffers in these judgments.

Eternal judgment is not established for the body but for the soul of man,*"tribulation and anguish, upon every soul of man that doeth evil, of the Jew first, and also of the Greek"* (Romans 2:9). Let us not think in terms of the body. As those who receive life will have a body prepared for eternal life, so will there be one for those who are judged for the second death (Hell Fire). Hell is often pictured with these present bodies which will not be the case. Ultimately, our current bodies will return to the dust from which it came. In the case of those in the first resurrection, the Scriptures say that the new body or house will be given at the appearing of Jesus. Nothing is said concerning the physical condition of those who are sentenced to the fires of Hell. The only indicator seems to be the parable of the rich man who asked for Abraham to bring some water to cool his tongue for he was "tormented in that place". Since Hell was made for the Devil and his angels (Matthew 25:41), who are spirits without tangible bodies as we are. They are to suffer eternal torment (Matthew 8:29), then it is possible for the wicked to be judged and suffer in a similar form. When the term "destroyed" is used in connection with eternal judgment it does not mean annihilation for a space of time. Remember, judgment is dealing with souls and not bodies.

There are ample Scriptures to support the fact that the wicked will suffer extreme torment forever and ever (Revelation 20:10). This judgment will take place at the "Great White Throne"

(Revelation 20:11) but will not include those of the first resurrection. The church will be with the judge (Jesus) and will actually make up God's throne. *"But the Lord shall endure forever, He has prepared his throne [church] for judgment"* (Psalm 9:7; 1 Corinthians 6:2). God will be the final judge and there are no appeals to this judgment. The record of each life will be presented and from those records every soul will be judged and given either life or death.

Judgment: Make a Distinction Between Entities

- Hebrews 9:27: God has appointed man once to die after that the judgment.
- Revelation 20:1-15: Those who are judged in the second resurrection.
- Matthew 13:49: The judgment of the righteous and wicked.
- Matthew 25:31-46: Before Him was gathered all nations to be judged.
- Matthew 18:7-9: Everlasting fire and Hell are the same things.
- Mark 9:42-48: Hellfire is not to be quenched and the worm (soul) never die.
- Isaiah 5:14: Hell has enlarged itself without measure.
- Isaiah 30:33 Hell is ordained of old.
- Matthew 25:41: Hell is prepared for the devil and his angels.
- Matthew 8:29: Have you (Jesus) come to torment us before our time?
- 2 Peter 2:4-9: The wicked angels are reserved to judgment (Jude v. 6).
- Isaiah 66:24: Those that are saved, will see the tormented bodies of the wicked in Hell.

- 2 Thessalonians 1:9-10: Those that trouble you are punished with everlasting destruction.
- Revelation 21:8 Who shall have part in the second death?
- Psalm 9:7 The wicked are turned into Hell.
- Romans 2:2; 5-8 The judgment of God is according to truth.
- Matthew 25:41; 25:46 Everlasting fire and everlasting punishment.
- Matthew 10:14-15 Those judged at Sodom and Gomorrah are better off than those who reject truth.
- Daniel 12:2 Some will be raised to everlasting contempt.
- Matthew 3:12 The fan is in His hand and He will burn the chaff with unquenchable fire.
- Acts 17:31 There is coming a day when Christ will judge the world in righteousness.
- Acts 24:25 Paul reasoned concerning the judgment to come.
- Mark 16:16 Those who believe not will be damned.
- Hebrews 10:26-27 If one sins will fully look for judgment and fiery indignation.
- Romans 2:2-16 The soul is the object of judgment.
- Matthew 13:30; 13:40-50 Angels to gather the tares and burn them with fire.
- Revelation 14:9-11 How long is Hell? Forever and forever-eternal.
- Revelation 22:14-15 Eternal judgment for those who do not keep His commandments.
- Job 21:30 The wicked reserved for the Day of Judgment.

- Matthew 7:22-23 Many will say in that day, Lord, Lord! He will say depart you workers of iniquity.

Outer Darkness, Term Used in Place of Hell or Eternal Separation from God

- Matthew 22:11-13: Bind him, cast into outer darkness.
- Matthew 24:48; 24:51: The portion of hypocrites, weeping and gnashing of teeth. The unfaithful servant (Job 8:13).
- Luke 12:46: Unfaithful servant's portion with the unbelievers and beaten with many stripes.
- Matthew 25:30: The unprofitable servant in outer darkness.
- Matthew 13:42: Children of kingdom rejected and cast into outer darkness.
- Matthew 8:12: The tears and the children of the kingdom.
- Matthew 23:33: The damnation of Hell.

The Second Death

The church and those in the first resurrection will have no part of being judged at the White Throne of Judgment but will join Christ and participate in the jugement process (Revelation 19:2; 20:6).

- Revelation 20:6: The second death has no power over those in the first resurrection.
- Romans 2:5-6: God to render to all according to the deeds done in the body (this life).
- John 5:29: Those who have done good given life and those with evil.
- Ecclesiastes 12:14: God to judge the secrets of men's hearts.

- Psalm 62:12: God will render to every man according to his works.
- Revelation 20:12: Dead are judged from the book according to works.
- Revelation 22:12: The reward will be according as their works shall be.

The judgment at the eternal bar of divine justice will be according to the deeds done in this life. *"For God will bring every work into judgment, with every secret thing, whether it be good, or whether it be evil"* (Ecclesiastes 12:14). *"Who will render to every man according to his deeds"* (Romans 2:6). *"The dead were judged out of those books, according to their works"* (Revelation 20:12). *"And, behold, I come quickly and my reward is with me, to give every man according as his work shall be"* (Revelation 22:12).

If one's deeds and works are to be judged, then there must be some standard by which deeds can be justly evaluated (Acts 17:31). Someone who does not know nor understand the human condition could not fairly judge our condition. Jesus came into the world and was tempted in the flesh, but remained sinless, providing a way for us to boldly come before Him and find grace to help in our time of need. Therefore, this firsthand knowledge of man's experiences and temptations qualifies Him to judge any men.

- Hebrews 4:15: He was tempted in all points as we are, yet without sin.
- 2 Thessalonians 1:6-10: Those who reject are punished with fire.
- Mark 16:16: The unbeliever is to be damned.
- John 5:22; 5:27: Judgment given to the sonto execute.
- Acts 10:42: Jesus to judge the living and dead (2 Timothy 4:1; 1 Peter 4:5).
- Acts 17:31: God has appointed a day to judge by Jesus Christ.

- Daniel 7:9-10: Man to be judged by the ancient of days (God).
- Jude (v. 7) The destruction of Sodom and Gomorrah are examples of Hell.

The conclusions we draw from the doctrine of eternal judgment are: Hell was not originally created for man but for the Devil and his angels. Hell has enlarged itself to accommodate the vast majority of mankind to this eternal place of destruction. Those who live ungodly and reject Jesus Christ as their saviour will be judged by the righteous standards of a just and Holy God through Jesus Christ, the Judge of all men. This judgment setting is called the "Great White Throne of Judgment". The church consist of those who make up His throne and will confirm the judgment that will be assigned. There will be two classes of men judged, the just and the unjust. Each group will be judged according to their works or deeds done in their life. The wicked will be sentenced to eternal damnation and will be tormented in the fires of Hell forever with no appeal or deliverance. This judgment is final.

Those who are judged worthy of life, whose names are written in the Lamb's Book of Life will be delivered from this "second death" and will live eternally with God some place in Heaven. God has a set of books where the deeds of man are recorded and the main volume is the "Word of God". The blessed and holy are those of the first resurrection. They will not be judged at this judgment setting. The judgment of those who will be counted as part of the first resurrection are currently being judged through the perfecting process of the New Testament church (the saints) (1 Peter 4:17-18).

These principles of the doctrine of Christs are the foundation for going onto perfection. To be perfect, one must know the will of God and be obedient to practice His will all our saved days on earth. From these precepts we believe the full doctrine of Christ will be revealed as an expansion for our growth and maturity in Him. It is not His will that we remain little children or babes in Christ, but to grow into the full stature of the mature man as demonstrated by the example set before us by Jesus Christ our Lord (Ephesians 4:13).

~9~
STRIVING FOR PERFECTION

Therefore leaving the principles of the doctrine of Christ, let us go onto perfection; not laying again the foundation of repentance from dead works, and faith toward God.

-- Hebrews 6:1

It is not God's purpose that we continue to build the foundation, but to build on the foundation that has already been established. The foundation is very important, but the objective is to build a house to serve the needs of the builder. After a child is born, the expectation is for him or her to grow and eventually come to maturity or full growth. When we have responded to the basic principles of the doctrine by being baptized and filled with the Holy Ghost, we are to begin building our "house" by living by the teachings of Jesus Christ and the apostles. How can perfection be defined? It is subduing the members of our body to obey God's word and do His will. The more we learn and practice His will, the greater our ability to master and do His will. *"But I keep under my body, and bring it into subjection: lest by any means, when I have preached to others, I myself should become a castaway"* (1 Corinthians 9:27). In other words, bringing our conduct into harmony with the life of Christ (Galatians 2:20).

The Goals of Perfection

1. To come to the unity of the faith.
2. To acquire a knowledge of the Son of God.
3. To come to the stature of a 'full grown man'.
4. To arrive at the measure of the full stature of Christ, the perfect man.
5. To bring forth fruit of righteousness that is pleasing to God.

In Hebrews 6:1, the word perfection comes from a family of Greek words which means to complete, completion, full growth, and maturity. This text refers to the act of being completed, which infers that up to this point man is an incomplete entity. What makes man imperfect? Sin and a lack of knowledge concerning the will of God. The only means of perfection available to the Jews was the Old Testament laws. The Gentiles had nothing and were without hope or any knowledge of God's promises (Ephesians 2:11-13).

God's purpose for man was for him to be holy and sinless. The only hope for man to become complete is in Christ (the church). *"According as he has chosen us in him before the foundation of the world, that we should be holy and without blame before him in love"* (Ephesians 1:4). The law given to Israel was only a schoolmaster to bring them to Christ, but it was not the perfecting force to make them holy (Galatians 3:24-25) *"For the law made nothing perfect, but the bringing in of a better hope did, by which we draw nigh unto God"* (Hebrews 7:19).

The complete man is one who has life. Mankind is born into sin and trespasses, has no life and therefore is not complete as God desired him to be. Efforts to live righteously under the Mosaic Law failed miserably, which caused Paul to comment

For if there had been a law given which could have given life, verily righteousness should have been by the law. But the scripture has concluded all under sin [dead], that the promise by faith of Jesus Christ might be given to them that believe (Galatians 3:21-22).

Eternal life comes from Christ, and if one is to reach full growth, that life must reside in Him, producing fruit to the glory of Jesus Christ. Full growth is fulfilling the righteousness of God as produced by His Spirit (John 15:4-5).

Before man can become a complete entity, sin must be removed from his life and he must be justified by the blood of Christ, so he can remain in the presence of God without condemnation. The Levitical Law system of blood sacrifice could not remove sin from the worshipper. The best the Jews could expected was the covering of sin until the next sacrifice was offered. The law gave knowledge of sin and what God's righteousness consisted of, but offered no help to perform the righteousness.

Therefore by the deeds of the law there shall no flesh be justified in his sight: for by the law is the knowledge of sin. But now the righteousness of God without the law is manifested, being witnessed by the law and prophets; even the righteousness of God which is by faith of Jesus Christ unto all and upon all them that believe: for there is no difference: for all have sinned, and come short of the glory of God, being justified freely by his grace through the redemption that is in Christ Jesus (Romans 3:20-24).

Perfection comes by faith in and obedience to Jesus Christ and His shed blood. Only the blood of Jesus can remove sin from the Jews and Gentiles. The hope of the Jews was in the blood of 'bulls and goats' which could not remove sin (Hebrews 10:4), but our hope (Jews and Gentiles) is in Christ and the work accomplished for our perfection on the cross of Calvary. *"Neither by the blood of bulls and calves, but by his own blood He entered in once into the holy place, having obtained eternal redemption for us"* (Hebrews 9:12). In Christ and only in Christ can man become the complete entity God purposed to have. When sin has been removed from the life of man, he is expected to proceed to full maturity. Scripture says all one needs are in

Christ and that *"we are complete in him, which is the head of all principality and power"* (Colossians 2:9-10). There is a standard of perfection and that is Jesus Christ, the perfect man, and the aim of every child of God is to emulate His life and to walk in His footsteps (Psalm 37:37; Ephesians 4:11-14; 1 John 2:6; 1 Peter 2:21).

Perfection as it has been expressed in past biblical times (dispensations) was dependent on the knowledge of God's will and purpose available at the time. The first reference to perfection was Enoch, who walked with God and pleased Him to the point that God took him (Genesis 5:24; Hebrews 11:5). The next person was Noah, who was perfect in his generations, and found grace in the eyes of God. He was used to save eight souls to re-populate the world following the flood. We all owe our existence to the faith of Noah (Genesis 6:9). Certainly, the perfection of Noah does not measure to the standards of this day except for the faith Noah had in God's word. Also, Job was deemed perfect and upright with God. *"Have you considered my servant Job?"* (Job 1:1; 1:8). Again, Job's perfection would not be sufficient for today's standards.

The march toward perfection and a perfect day is clearly seen in the Book of Ezekiel in what is known as Ezekiel's river (Ezekiel 47:1-5). The waters (the knowledge of God's will and purpose) began under the threshold of the human family (Adam) and streamed from the righteous line of Seth. It continues for 1,000 cubits (years) with waters only up to the ankles. It goes on for another 1,000 cubits where it reaches to the knees. It flows until it reaches the loins. Finally, after 4,000 cubits (years), it becomes a river to swim in (the full knowledge of God's will and purpose). This 4,000 years covers the time from Adam to Christ and unfolds the progressive revelation of God's will to the dawn of a more perfect day. This better day is the advent of Christ, where the full knowledge of God is made known. It is at this point, for the first time in man's existence, that he could be purged from sin and uncleanness with the hope of being filled with the divine nature of God (the Holy Ghost). The progress of Ezekiel's river reveals the progressive revelation of man's perfecting process with first a small knowledge of God's will at Enoch's translation (Hebrews 11:5). The next level is at the birth and calling of Abraham, on through the giving of the Levitical Law, and then to the temple (God's house). The prophets revealed more and more of God's purpose through their prophecies and gave detailed accounts of the coming Messiah, Jesus Christ. The water to swim in, represents the church age, the day of grace, where the full revelation of Christ and the movement of His Spirit is centered in the New Testament church.

The next step in 'Going Onto Perfection' is maturity, progressing from babies in Christ to full growth as mature sons of God.

> *For when for the time ye ought to be teachers, you have need that one teach you again which be the first principles of the oracles of God; and are become such as have need of milk, and not strong meat, For every one that useth milk is unskillful in the word of righteousness: for he is a babe. But strong meat belongeth to them that are of full age, even those who by reason of use have their senses exercised to discern both good and evil (Hebrews 5:12-14).*

As children of God, we are expected to grow from babies, with a limited knowledge and understanding of God's word to being able to master the 'strong doctrine', and being able to teach others the ways of God. To live as servants of God is more than just 'repent, be baptized, and filled with the Holy Ghost'. The knowledge of God's word and its application to our lives is essential to the productive service in God's kingdom. The Holy Ghost coupled with true teaching is needed to rightly divide the Word of Truth. Strong meat is that portion of God's word that digs deep into our lives and reveals the hidden purpose of His will.

> *All scripture is by inspiration of God, and is profitable for doctrine [teaching], for reproof [admonish and chastise],*

> *for correction [to put back on the right track] and for instruction in righteousness; that the man of God may be perfect [complete], thoroughly furnished unto good works (2 Timothy 3:16-17).*

Titus (2:1-15) provides a sample of strong meat. Holiness is the standard of perfection because it replicates the life of Christ. Without holiness, one cannot please God (Hebrews 12:14). All of the New Testament epistles (letters to the churches) contain instructions needed to fulfill the requirements of holiness and holy living. God, from the beginning, has demanded fruit from His children. God's disappointment with Israel was their failure to produce righteous fruit and they only brought forth wild grapes (Isaiah 5:1-7). John chapter 15, Jesus refers to Himself as the true vine and we as the branches are expected to bear fruit. If the branch fails to produce fruit, it is cut off and burned. Jesus, on one occasion, approached a fig tree expecting to find figs and there were none. As a result, the tree was cursed (Mark 11:13-21). Israel referred to as a fig tree and also an olive tree. In Romans 11:11-25, the natural branches of the olive tree (Israel) are broken off and the 'wild olive branch' (Gentiles) is grafted in and expected to bring forth good fruit. The root cause was Israel's lack of faith. Without faith, there can be no productivity or spiritual growth.

> *But God be thanked, that ye were the servant of sin, but ye have obeyed from the heart that form of doctrine which was delivered you. Being then made free from sin ye became the servant of righteousness. I speak after the manner of men because of the infirmity of your flesh: for as ye have yielded your members servants to uncleanness and to iniquity unto iniquity; even so now yield your members servants to righteousness unto Holiness (Romans 6:17-19).*

Fruit is the principle product of the tree and vine. If that fruit does not come to maturity, it is useless and unfit to eat. In the growing process, many things can hinder the development of the fruit including disease, injury, lack of moisture, poor soil, and weeds, which can hinder growth and cause the tree to lose its value. The parable of the sower illustrates the word planted in the heart, which was choked with riches, pleasures, and the cares of life, "*and bring no fruit to perfection*" (Luke 8:14). However, the good ground, representing the honest and good heart, heard and retained the Word and brought forth fruit with patience (v. 15)

Growth is a progressive process and it occurs in small increments at a time. Growth may not be noticed in one day, but adding many days will ensure a noticeable change. One does not advance from the first grade to high school overnight. It takes time to master the knowledge and experience necessary to be promoted. One can be perfect at a given stage of life, that is measuring up to expected accomplishment at that stage, while at the same time moving toward full growth. It has been said that 'we are perfect while being perfected'. As babies in Christ, the fundamentals have been learned, but how to use those fundamentals take time and teaching.

Ye therefore, beloved, seeing ye know these things before, beware lest ye also, being led away with the error of the wicked, fall from your steadfastness. But grow in grace, and in the knowledge of our Lord and Saviour Jesus Christ. To him be glory both now and forever (2 Peter 3:17-18).

As one grows in Christ, they are able to withstand the attacks of Satan more easily and overcome the temptations around them. Babies are easily hurt, but full grown men can take a lot of abuse and not be destroyed by it. Learning how to control our desires by surrendering to the will of God is a measure of perfection. Apostle Paul states,

For we know in part, and we prophesy in part, but when that which is perfect comes, then that which is in part shall be done away. When I was a child, I spake as a child, I understood as a child, I thought as a child: but when I became a man, I put away childish things (1 Corinthians 13:9-11).

Teaching and learning is an absolute necessity to reach full growth (Colossians 2:6-8). Knowing truth is the only way to escape the deceptive practices of the deceiver. To know truth, one must be taught truth. *"My people are destroyed for lack of knowledge"* (Hosea 4:6). Self-taught people are, as a rule, poorly taught. A child in school will not learn the proper lesson if there is no teacher. Neither can the children of God advance spiritually without sound doctrine. Going onto maturity requires a teacher who knows what they are teaching (Hebrews 5:13-14). A full grown person is stable and unmovable in their place. We are to be rooted and grounded in truth and unmoved for the hope of the gospel (Colossians 1:22-23). When storms come through tests and adversities, one will not be moved from their foundation in Christ. When the winds of false doctrine blow toward us, we will not be affected because of the principle of truth in us. Our stability in Christ is the result of the God given ministry which is provided for our security and growth. *"There will henceforth be no more children, tossed to and fro, and carried about with every wind and doctrine, by the slight of men, and cunning craftiness, whereby they lie in wait to deceive"* (Ephesians 4:14; Colossians 2:6-9).

Maturity consists of many things: knowledge, understanding, living the life of Christ, overcoming and mastering temptations, and doing those things which are right and pleasing in the sight of God. *"Having therefore these promises, dearly beloved, let us cleanse ourselves from all filthiness of the flesh and spirit, perfecting holiness in the fear of God"* (2 Corinthians 7:1). To be complete, there are responsibilities an individual must perform if perfection is to be attained. The above verse teaches one to cleanse themselves from all filthiness of the flesh and spirit. The Book of Colossians (3:5) informs us to mortify our corrupt deeds and the Book of Ephesians (4:22) admonishes to do away with the former conversation [manner of life] of the old man, which is corrupt according to the deceitful lust; and be renewed in the spirit of your mind; and that ye put on the new man, which after God is created in righteousness and true holiness. The old man is dismissed and the new man is invited in. The command is to *"walk in the Spirit, and ye shall not fulfill the lust of the flesh"* (Galatians 5:16). Maturity then, is walking in the Spirit under the control of the Holy Ghost, and not according to the will or desires of the flesh (vs. 19-24). Essentially, exemplify the difference between fleshly desires and the fruit of the Spirit as God requires.

While going onto perfection requires discipline and submission on the part of the individual; however, it is now left entirely up to the person. God must be part of the process of assisting and giving strength to proceed on the path to perfection.

> *That he would grant you, according to the riches of his glory, to be strengthened in the inner man; that Christ may dwell in your hearts by faith; that ye being rooted and grounded in love, may be able to comprehend with all saints what is the breath, and length, and depth, and height; and to know the love of Christ, which passes knowledge, that ye might be filled with all the fullness of God. Now unto him that is able to do exceeding abundantly above all that we ask or think, according to the power that worketh in us"* (Ephesians 3:16-20).

"For it is God which worketh in you both to will and do of his good pleasure" (Philippians 2:13). Further, *"we are his workmanship, created in Christ Jesus unto good works, which God hath before ordained that we should walk in them"* (Ephesians 2:10). Without faith in Christ, perfection is impossible. It is perfecting the work of charity, God's divine love works through individuals (1 Corinthians 13). Growth is adding to what presently exists. One is to add to their faith, virtue, knowledge, temperance, patience, godliness, brotherly, kindness, and lastly, charity. *"For if these things be in you, and abound, they make you that ye shall neither be barren nor unfruitful in the knowledge of our Lord Jesus Christ"* (2 Peter 1:8).

The subject of going onto perfection is applied to one who has been delivered from sin and filled with the Spirit of Life, thus putting them on the path to become a complete man as God would have them to be. This complete man lives the life of Christ, who is the standard of perfection, and with His Spirit produces the fruit of righteousness. One begins their life in Christ as a babe but is expected in time to advance to full growth so they can teach others the ways of God. Spiritual growth and maturity is dependent on one's knowledge of God as applied in life. This knowledge must be taught and does not come automatically because one is saved. The evidence of growth is measured by the fruit one bears. The fruit of righteousness is the harvest God is expecting, but without fruit, the tree (one's life) is of no value to God. Jesus Christ is the source of our help and the object of our affections. Without Him, there is no growth. Faith in His Word, a knowledge of His will along with the willingness to obey His commandments are the keys to a perfect life in Christ. God has provided a staff of ministry for the feeding of His people and the perfecting of the saints.

Spiritual growth is manifested in subduing the desires of the flesh and walking under the control of the Spirit. To do so is life. The following list of additional Scriptures are provided to aid in further research and knowledge of the process of perfection. These epistles do not teach theory, but the requirement of a practical day to day conduct expected of a growing, mature child of God.

- Peter 1:12: Established in the present truth.
- Psalm 37:37: Mark the perfect man, the end is peace.
- Psalm 19:7: The Law of the Lord makes wise the simple.
- Ephesians 4:11-13: The ministry is God's gift for the perfecting of the saints.
- Colossians 1:9-11: We might be filled with the knowledge of His will, walking to please Him.
- 1Thessalonians 4:1: Instructed that you might know how to please God.

- Romans 12:2: Be not conformed to this world, but be transformed.
- Romans 13:14: Make no provisions for the flesh to fulfill its desires.
- Hebrews 12:1: Lay aside every weight and run with patience this race.
- Philippians 3:11-15: We are not perfect now, but we press forward to the prize.
- James 1:4: Let patience have its perfect work.
- 1 Corinthians 3:1-3: I could not speak unto you as spiritual, but as babes (immature). Why?
- Isaiah 28:9: To whom shall we teach doctrine? Those drawn from the breast.
- Proverbs 4:18: The path of the just a shining light, shining unto a more perfect day.
- I John 3:3: He that has this hope (to be like Jesus) purifieth himself as He is pure.
- 1 Corinthians 9:27: I bring under my body with its desires.
- Colossians 1:28: We warn and teach all men to present themselves perfect in Christ.
- Philippians 1:9-10: Approve things that are excellent.
- I Peter 5:10: After we have suffered, make perfect, strengthen and settle us.
- Hebrews 2:10: He learned obedience by the things he suffered (Hebrews 5:8).
- Philippians 1:6: He that has begun a good work in you will finish it.
- Colossians 4:12: Labor in prayers that you stand perfect and complete in the will of God.

- Galatians 2:20: The life I now live in Christ I live by faith of Jesus Christ.
- 1 Peter 2:2: Desire the sincere milk of the word that you may grow thereby.
- Jeremiah 3:15: Give pastors who will feed you with knowledge and understanding.

As full grown saints, our task is to work in God's vineyard to produce the fruit of righteousness for others to see and glorify God. We are to bring souls into the church where the gospel will convict and draw them with cords of love. We ourselves are to be examples of true believers giving the world a contrast between those who possess the Spirit of Christ and those who do not. Only by our obedience to His will and grace can this be accomplished.

AUTHOR

Dr. Harry L. Herman was born in Indianapolis, Indiana, Nov. 14, 1924. He was baptized in the name of Jesus and filled with the Holy Ghost on July 5th, 1949 and raised in Christ Temple, Indianapolis. Later, he served in the U.S. army in the Pacific Ocean theatre in World War II.

On October 9, 1949, he married Jenny Rea "Jerry" Herman, and the Lord blessed them with 5 sons. Bishop Herman and Dr. Jerry were active members of Christ Temple. He served in almost every department of the church and in 1960-1965, he served as Assistant Pastor. He was called to pastor Christ Temple in Detroit, Michigan. He received his ministerial fellowship certificate in March 1955 with the A.B.S.A. Ultimately, he became the chairman of the Sunday School Department and the assistant chairman of the Young People's Department in the A.B.S.A.

He was elevated to the Bishopric in the Pentecostal Assemblies of the World, Inc. in March 1989 and consecrated in August 1989. He currently serve as an emeritus member of the Board of Bishops. He has served on many committees: the Pulpit Committee, License & Credential Committee, Chairman and member of the Judicial Committee, and Director of the I.C.E.A. He is a well-known Bible teacher who stands firmly on the Pentecostal Apostolic message. He received his early teaching from his parents, who received their instructions from the late Bishop G. T. Haywood, and Elder Robert F. Tobin. His ministry was further enhanced by reading Bishop Haywood's writings and sitting under the late Bishop Morris E. Golder, and the late

Bishop Willie Lee. He served as Diocesan of the Minnesota, Wisconsin, and Dakotas Council for nearly seven years before being appointed Diocesan of the Northern District Council March (Michigan) from 1996-2013. He was elected Chairman of the Council in 1984 for two terms and served as District Elder for 11 years.

He moved his family to Kalamazoo at the invitation of the late Bishop Ross P. Paddock in September 1970 to become the Assistant Pastor of Christ Temple in Kalamazoo, Michigan. Bishop Paddock resigned June 5, 1972 as Pastor and Dr. Harry Herman was elected the Pastor, faithfully serving until January 31, 2010. He has a perfect record in Sunday School for 34 years as a teacher. He received an honorary Doctor of Divinity from the Aenon Bible College in 1994. He earned a Doctor of Theology and a Doctor of Divinity in 1995 from the International Apostolic College. He is an esteemed counselor and teacher of young ministers, pastors, and married couples.

AFTERWORD

The principles of this book have been applied in the church where the author pastored. They lead to the development of the members and ultimately to the growth of his congregation. These principles were instrumental in establishing the leadership of the church and directing the vision of the ministry. This study guide of these principles is written as a teaching tool for those new to the faith and aspiring young ministers to understand the fundamentals of the precious Pentecostal Oneness message we cherish. It is important to know the truth before one can teach it.

NOTES

A Concise History of the Early Church by Norbert Box, 1996.

A History of Christian Thought by Arthur Cushman McGiffert, 1954.

A Reader in Pentecostal Theology: Voices from the First Generation edited by Douglas Gordon Jacobsen, 2006

Dispensational Truth by Clarence Lakin.

Fox's Book of Martyrs edited by Williams Byron Forbush.

"God", *The HarperCollins Encyclopedia of Catholicism.*

Greek-English Lexicon of the New Testament by Grimm-Thayer.

Studies in Christian Antiquity, 1985.

The Birth of the Spirit by Garfield Thomas Haywood.

The Doctrine of Unconditional Eternal Security Fact or Fallacy by Bishop Earl Parchia.

The Early Church by Henry Chaswick, 1993.

The Resurrection of the Dead by Garfiel Thomas Haywood.

The Principles of the Doctrine of Christ by Robert F. Tobin.

The Seven Stages Of The First Resurrection by Ross Perry Paddock.

The Story of Civilization: The Age of Faith, Vol. 4, 1950.

The Victim of the Flaming Sword by Garfield Thomas Haywood.

Vine's Complete Expository Dictionary: Of Old and New Testament Words by W E. Vine.

www.ingramcontent.com/pod-product-compliance
Lightning Source LLC
LaVergne TN
LVHW041547070426
835507LV00011B/962